D1235922

CONFLICT
AND
SOCIAL CHANGE

CONFLICT AND SOCIAL CHANGE

BY MARCUS BORG

AUGSBURG PUBLISHING HOUSE
Minneapolis, Minnesota

LIBRARY — LUTHERAN SCHOOL
OF THEOLOGY AT CHICAGO

HN
17.5
.B66

CONFLICT AND SOCIAL CHANGE

Copyright © 1971 Augsburg Publishing House

Library of Congress Catalog Card No. 74-135220

International Standard Book Number 0-8066-9461-0

All rights reserved. No part of this book may be used or reproduced in any manner whatsoever without written permission except in the case of brief quotations in critical articles and reviews. For information address Augsburg Publishing House, 426 South Fifth Street, Minneapolis, Minnesota 55415.

Scripture quotations are from the Revised Standard Version of the Bible, copyright 1946 and 1952 by the Division of Christian Education of the National Council of Churches, and from the New English Bible, copyright 1961 by Oxford University Press, and are used by permission.

Manufactured in the United States of America

CONTENTS

THE PROBLEM: RAPID CHANGE AND CONFLICT

Only the very young know this world as natives know their own country; the rest of us are like immigrants recently arrived, feeling our way in a strange land. One thing about it is certain: change — constant, irresistible, rapid, and pervasive change. This is the first characteristic of man's communities all over the world.[1]

The above claim of anthropologist Margaret Mead seems to be an overstatement; for, if taken seriously, it means that most of the readers of this book, and the author, are really strangers in this world. What is most important, however, is to note the reason which Dr. Mead gives for the strangeness of the world: it is changing so rapidly. For this book seeks to examine change and the role of conflict in change, and to develop a theological framework within which to understand and evaluate social change and conflict.

The world is changing constantly, radically, and irresistibly, but, depending on where we live and what activities occupy most of our time, it is relatively easy to be unaware, or at best dimly aware, of the dramatic changes that have occurred, are occurring, and are expected to occur. For example, these words are being written in a university setting more than 700 years old; from within these ancient buildings, it is easy to imagine that the fundamental character of the world is stability and permanence rather than change. Similarly, the common centers of our lives suggest that stability and permanence, or at most moderate change, are the essential character of our existence. In our local churches, we use liturgies and hymns that have undergone but moderate change in our lifetimes. Our homes are often viewed as rather unchanging centers of security that give stability to our lives regardless of what happens "out there." Our planning for old age also seems to assume that the world will be much the same then as now, except for a bit of anticipated inflation. Thus several common experiences lead us to think that stability is the essence of our lives. Consequently, it is necessary to be more specific in claiming that change, not stability, is "the first characteristic of man's communities all over the world."

In the following pages, several sources of social change are identified. It would be misleading to conceive of them as operating independently of each other, but for the sake of analysis they will be delineated separately.

TECHNOLOGY

Economist John Maynard Keynes stated that there have been two periods of rapid and dramatic social change in the history of man. The first probably occurred before the last ice age when man's primitive ingenuity gave rise to such discoveries as the domestication of fire, the wheel, the making of tools. The second, caused by the scientific and industrial revolutions, began in the last part of the 18th century and continues today. As a result, life in the last two centuries has changed and is still changing more basically than at any time since the beginning of recorded history.[2]

Simply to list some of the effects that technology has had on our personal and social lives drives this claim home.

AFFLUENCE is one result. Some readers of this book can recall the Depression, when it was a treat to receive an orange or basket of fruit as one's "big" Christmas present. Most readers of this book are now far beyond that stage, though tragically most of the world is not. Indeed, we have advanced so far that multi-colored sidewall tires for bicycles can now be presented in the advertising on children's television programs!

COMMUNICATION, typified by television, is another result. For the first time in the history of the world, we now know who all our neighbors are in the sense that no conflict or problem of the world's people is foreign to our living rooms. Needless to say, this creates new potentialities and responsibilities. On the other side of the coin, it was quite possible for a middle class child in the 1800s to mature without ever seeing a violent death; now our children see thousands of violent deaths on television before they are twelve. All the evidence for assessing the effect of this change is not yet in. Further, though the poor of the world frequently do not own television sets, through their access to the mass media they are aware of the great chasm between their subsistence level of living and the conspicuous consumption of the West. They know that most children in North America will have electric toothbrushes before their own children will have a daily glass of milk. The seeds of conflict are present.

MEDICAL TECHNOLOGY has advanced incredibly, relieving most of us in the wealthy nations from the fear of an early death due to disease. It has also created a new specter, overpopulation and famine, for population growth is exceeding economic growth in many areas of the developing world, and the effects are already being felt.

THE GHETTO, both in the U.S. and in other nations, has also been partially produced by technology. As agricultural efficiency has increased, the number of jobs available in rural areas has decreased. Couple that with the alleged availability of employment in industrial areas,

9

and the result is a mass migration of unskilled labor to major population centers. Unfortunately, technology also means that there is not much demand for unskilled labor, and so the net result is a growing nucleus of poverty in the central city, intensified by racism.

SEXUAL MORES, or at least behavior, have also been affected by technology. Popular sexual morality was often based on the triple terrors of infection, conception, and detection. Now the privacy of the car has eliminated some of the fear of detection, birth-control devices have eliminated the fear of conception, and modern drugs have eliminated the worst consequences of infection. Whether this change will lead to the total loss of norms for sexual behavior, or whether it will produce a sexual ethic based on devotion rather than dread remains to be seen. Clearly, though, change is inevitable.

WAR, and the traditional justification for it, has also been affected, or ought to be. There once was a time when wars could be fought for limited ends with limited means, and when non-combatants could be relatively safe. To be sure, there have always been barbarisms in war, but the notion of "total war," implying total participation by whole nations and the often unexpressed notion that anybody is a fair target for mass bombing raids and/or biological-chemical warfare, is a product of the 20th century. Clearly this is due to the development of military technology. Whether the changed methods of warfare can still be justified by norms that grew up in a less technological society is certainly an open question.

AUTOMATION AND CYBERNATION, the application of self-correcting machines and computers to production, also portend dramatic consequences. The first of these is an increasing amount of leisure, made possible by a dramatic reduction in the number of man-hours needed to produce the goods that we consume. Will we make creative use of that leisure? Or will we permit that decision to be made by the sophisticated advertising of a system which requires that we consume more and more products? Second is the psychological change which we will have to undergo to think of ourselves as consumers rather than producers; that is, what happens to the "vocation of work" in a society where consumers are needed

10

more than producers? Third is a probable necessity to rethink the means of distribution; that is, when a small percentage of the population can produce the goods we require, will it still be possible to distribute the benefits of the system primarily on the basis of how much work we've done? Or will technology "accidentally" produce the situation where something akin to a guaranteed annual wage, regardless of work performed, is a necessity and not only a political goal for some groups? Fourth, and probably most immediate, is the consequence that automation is having even now for unskilled workers. When most of our ancestors arrived in the U.S., a strong back was sufficient qualification for obtaining a job. But now, unskilled workers — especially in those minority groups who have been educationally deprived — find that a strong back is a very meager qualification in the "promised land" of urban industrial society.

The examples above are enough to show that technology is producing dramatic changes and situations that will call for further dramatic social change. Most of these changes have produced both immeasurable benefit and tragic complications. But no attempt is being made to bewail technology; surely no one wants to go back to that stage where half of the children could expect to die by age five because of childhood diseases. Rather, the claim is being advanced that technology, unless supremely well-guided, produces some changes which are intended, and some accidental changes which create the likelihood of conflict and the need for further change.

NEW SOCIAL IDEAS AND SOCIAL MOVEMENTS

The second major cause of social change in the last two hundred years, and of the "strangeness" of the world in which we live, is the emergence of several new social ideas, new in the sense that they are no longer thought of as unachievable dreams but have become incarnate in political and social movements. It is the incarnation of these ideas that constitutes the "new."

The first of these ideas is democratization as a practical political ideal. Perhaps the incarnation of this idea in a political movement should be credited to the American and French revolutions. These two upheavals destroyed the long-established understanding that kings and nobility ruled by "divine right," that the order of society is either ordained by a god or gods, or by some natural law that is unchangeable. Clearly, however, these two epoch-ending events proved that kings could in fact be eliminated, and that it was possible to create a new order of society. Initially, the revolutionary movement of the modern world appears to have been a middle-class movement against the nobility. In this century, it has increasingly become a movement of workers and dispossessed against systems that exclude them from the benefits of those systems. This "secularizing" of the political order, the notion that it is the task of man to shape the structures of society, not to mutely accept some divinely or naturally ordained system, has striking ramifications. Foremost is the insistence that no class or ethnic group or nation has an intrinsic right to rule others. This idea has become incarnate in the movements of former colonial people, women, students, and minority groups in the U.S. and elsewhere. Each of these groups has said, in effect, "Why should we as women accept a society ruled by men alone?" Or, "Why should we as Africans accept a society ruled by Europeans alone?" Or, as in the black power movement, "Why should black people accept a society ruled almost exclusively by whites?" It is clear that the process of democratization not only is a significant change from the conditions that preceded it, but is also a potent source of continuing change, of conflict between social groups, between the old and the new.

Second among the social ideas is the realization that poverty is not a necessary element in human existence. Earlier in history, the scarcity of food and manufactured goods meant that somebody had to be poor; there just wasn't enough to go around. (This may help to clarify the statement, "The poor you will always have with you"; in a time of economic scarcity, it is true.) Now modern methods of producing food mean that there *is* enough to go around, but people still starve because of the human failure to solve the problem of distribution. This new situation is pregnant with both potential and peril.

It means, on the one hand, that poverty can be eliminated. On the other hand, it means that the continued existence of poverty is intolerable, indefensible, and explosive. Poor people will no longer be persuaded that their poverty is from natural scarcity, but believe that it is caused by some malfunction of the structures of society, or to the greed and selfishness of the middle and upper classes. In the United States this idea has become incarnate several times, for example, in the labor movement and in the Poor People's Campaign. That the continued presence of poverty both nationally and internationally will continue to produce change and conflict needs no demonstration. How long, for example, can the present political and economic structures, both national and international, survive in a world where the economic gap between developed nations and the developing nations is actually becoming wider? Note that we are not asking at this point, "How much longer *ought* they survive?" Rather, the question is, "How much longer *can* they survive?"

An editorial in the WALL STREET JOURNAL describes the international dimension of this problem:

> To analysts such as Britain's [Barbara] Ward, the significance of such statistics is clear: the economic gap is rapidly widening "between a white, complacent, highly bourgeois, very wealthy, very small North Atlantic elite and everybody else, and this is not a very comfortable heritage to leave to one's children." "Everybody else" includes approximately two-thirds of the population of the earth, spread through about 100 nations. . . . Many diplomats and economists view the implications as overwhelmingly — and dangerously — political. Unless the present decline [in the relative position of the developing nations] can be reversed, these analysts fear, the United States and other wealthy industrial powers of the West face the distinct possibility, in the words of Miss Ward, "of a sort of international class war."[3]

The point is that change is inevitable, and probably conflict will accompany it; the *kind* of change, however, and the consequences of conflict, are not.

Third among the new social ideas is the one that sounds like a cliché: the claim that all men are created equal. This statement, embodied in the American Declaration of Independence and in other documents as well, has the most radical implications.[4] Imagine that you live in the 19th century, when the implications of this idea began to become clear. As you examine your society (e.g., Germany or England), you become immediately aware of appalling inequities. Conditions of housing, nutrition, disease, and employment for most of the society stagger the senses. How do you account for this? If you accept as part of your credo the claim that all men are created equal, then you cannot say, "It's because some people are naturally lazy, unambitious, or destined to be poor." Since you cannot use that explanation, the only possible alternative is to conclude that these deplorable inequities are caused by some fault in the structures of the society. If it is the structures that are at fault, then new or different structures ought to be able to ameliorate, if not totally correct, the grinding inequities. It is this discovery that has provided the passionate drive behind many movements, especially when coupled with the previous two ideas. Not only Marxist movements, but such modest innovations as child labor laws, social security, collective bargaining, and free education, owe their inception to such affirmations.

CHANGE AND CONFLICT

The combination of these ideas and movements, together with the technological impulses for change noted earlier, has produced an unstable situation which is producing conflict — wars of national liberation, black militancy, student protest — and will probably continue to do so. For one effect of this combination of pressures is to increase the expectations of oppressed groups throughout the world, to make them increasingly impatient with the stultifying physical, economic, and psychological conditions under which they and their children live.[5] Richard Shaull of Princeton Theological Seminary sums up the situation succinctly:

In a static society, where there are no . . . pressures for change, the problem of violence is usually not a serious or complicated one. But in a world in which people have awakened to hope, they are constantly pressing toward a new order that of necessity implies a "violation" of the old. As such expectancy becomes more universal, violence can be an important element, both in blocking change and in bringing it about.[6]

So great is the magnitude of change that many observers of the contemporary scene argue that we are living in the transition period between the modern world and some as yet unnamed world: the post-modern era. This means that some of the most-cherished phenomena of the old eon — Christendom, the dominance of western culture, capitalism, individualism — may be passing out of existence. It is not a question of whether or not we want change, or of whether or not there will be change. Change is inevitable. The real question is what *kind* of change is desirable, and how does one achieve it? This changing situation, which may be the end of an epoch, is accompanied by conflict, both actual and potential.

This combination of conflict and social change, the central social fact of our age, impels us to address the question of how the faithful community should react to and use change and conflict. The rest of this book seeks to examine that question.

BARRIERS TO UNDERSTANDING CONFLICT AND SOCIAL CHANGE

2

If you do not specify and confront real issues, what you do will surely obscure them. If you do not alarm anyone morally, you will yourself remain morally asleep. If you do not embody controversy, what you say will be an acceptance of the drift to the coming human hell.[1]

The imperative need for involvement in social change, conflict, and controversy is marvelously stated above. Yet, most of us probably find social change and conflict distasteful and unnerving. Rather than affirming the opening statement, our inclination is probably to second the comment of a truck driver in Hammond, Indiana:

Life is getting faster and furiouser. Sometimes you feel like throwing up your hands and saying to hell with it and going so far back in the hills they'll have to pipe sunshine in.[2]

Or, as one scholar puts it as he comments about the social conflict that invariably accompanies social change:

> To many, social conflict is a sign of trouble, something to avoid, to run away from, or to conceal because it is freighted with controversy.... Among American Christians the word "conflict" often carries with it a decidedly negative connotation.[3]

Why do we find it distasteful? And why does a consideration of the problems posed in the first chapter perhaps sound especially alien to Christian faithfulness? What, after all, does the church have to do with that? Anything?

Most readers of this book are both American and Christian and a variety of notions in this ethos stand as barriers to a useful understanding of change and conflict. Since this is a book which seeks to relate Christian faithfulness to change and conflict, we had best be as clear and honest as we can about those barriers.

RELIGIOUS BARRIERS

For Christians especially, one barrier is the familiar argument that the task of the church ought to be limited to serving individuals, that it has no responsibility for man's social, political, or economic affairs. When it does become involved, the argument continues, it inevitably sells out the gospel in a state of social concern, and causes dissension among its members. Such is the cost of meddling with matters that are not its proper concern.

This basic argument is expressed and fortified in many ways. We shall delineate five. First, it is claimed, the proper orientation of the church and the Christian is otherworldly; what is really important is not this world, but the eternal realm of heaven or, alternatively, the inner realm of the spirit. If this is the case, then the problems and joys of this world pale into insignificance, and social change, though it may be real, is not related to the core of the gospel.

Coupled with the focus on otherworldliness is a second barrier that we can label a "this-worldly pessimism." This widespread notion is that things never really change, at least not down deep; what has been will be, the poor you will always have with you, the future is closed, and there is nothing new under the sun. So it really doesn't make sense to get too bound up with the problems of earth, or with trying to bring about change. The doctrine of original sin is often pressed into service here as well. Since there is a basic flaw in man's nature, it is affirmed, we can never achieve individual or societal perfection this side of eternity, so efforts designed to radically change society are dismissed as utopian.

A third barrier contributing to the notion that Christian faithfulness has little or nothing to do with social and political matters is the slogan—almost a sacred dogma—"separation of church and state." What the originators of this statement intended is that Congress should not establish any religion or denomination as the state-supported religion. But in the popular mind, the transition is readily made from "separation of church and state" to "separation of religion and politics." "Religion and politics don't mix," is the strident cry, and what God — or the Founding Fathers — put asunder, let not man join together.

That American Christians have successfully separated religion from politics has been demonstrated by study after study. A few examples will suffice.

In a survey of church members in a Midwestern county with a high-percentage of church membership, it was discovered that fewer than five people out of a sample of 1200 church members related their Christian faith to economic or political questions.[4] Of the Lutheran congregations surveyed, 0 percent in one congregation were aware of any political or social statement made by the denomination, and only 12 percent in another congregation knew of even one such statement.[5] The authors of this study concluded:

> Only in a very few cases did respondents in any of the traditions extant in Corn County reveal any self-conscious reflection on the issue of the relationship between the church and the world.[6]

This conviction that religion and politics don't mix is well expressed by an angry church member whose pastor had apparently begun to "mix" religion and politics by speaking of the Mexican-American grapeworkers' protest against working conditions in California:

> I used to go to church and the preacher would talk about God, Jesus, and the Bible. Now he tells me why I shouldn't buy grapes.[7]

His disgruntlement is in fact justified by the notions that we have examined thus far. If they are correct, then he is right in thinking that the church ought have nothing to say about such earthly matters. Clearly this separation of religion and politics is a major barrier to understanding Christian faithfulness in the midst of change.

A fourth belief operative in our ethos is that one of the main gifts bestowed by the Christian faith is "peace of mind." Not only do titles of recent popular religious books suggest this, but the rhetoric of tranquility, serenity, peace, and psychological well-being as fruits of religious faith reinforces this sentiment. It is well-illustrated by comments from parishioners: I go to church because "it gives me peace of mind. I feel relieved when I go to church." [8] Or, another parishioner complained because his pastor raised disturbing questions: "I know that I do not come to church to be disturbed. I get enough of that in downtown Chicago during the week." [9] One suspects that the quest after "peace of mind" is so strong that God is relegated to the position of being but a means to an end, as a means to my psychological well-being. But this quest after peace of mind virtually excludes any significant involvement in social change or conflict. For if peace of mind is a primary goal of the Christian, rapid change, conflict, or any other force disrupting peace of mind is clearly hostile to Christianity.

Fifth and finally, among those ideas which support Christian non-involvement in social and political questions is a particular interpretation of an isolated passage from St. Paul: "Let every person be subject to the governing authorities. For there is no authority except from God, and those that exist have been instituted by God" (Rom. 13:1). This verse, taken out of its historic context and separated from Paul's understanding of authorities and powers, is often quoted to suggest that the

19

basic duty of the Christian toward the social and political order is to obey it, not change it! Thus this passage gives many Christians what they regard as a solid reason to endorse the status quo, to be a good citizen, always obedient to law. To such a person, conflict and radical change can only appear as a threat to a divinely established system of authority and order.

CULTURAL BARRIERS

In addition to these five religious barriers several cultural factors also limit our ability to understand change. First among these is a strong preference for harmony, stability, and order. To be realistic, it is doubtful that anybody could remain sane for long without some degree of order. But it is possible to have an inordinate preference for harmony coupled with a disproportionate fear of conflict. Most of us from our childhood were taught to value harmony and dislike conflict, no matter how many feelings we might have to repress in order to avoid conflict. One might almost say that we were taught to place a higher value on the most hate-filled harmony than on an honest conflict carried on in a spirit of love. So also in marriages: many couples value a superficial harmony so much that conflict, no matter how helpful it might be, is avoided. Typical is this fragment of a conversation with a distraught husband:

> Don't send us to a marriage guidance counsellor. We have been, and frankly I was dismayed. We told him we had never had a row in our twelve years of marriage, and he said he thought this was a pity and that things might have gone better if we had. I think this was a wicked thing to say, as I strongly disapprove of strife.

Extended to the social scene, it is easy to see that such a high valuation of harmony and stability is not likely to make one open to social change and conflict.

A second culturally induced barrier is the strong strand of individualism in American culture. Most of us take great pride in pointing to our accomplishments and

20

being able to say, "*I* did that," whether the accomplishment is a certain income level, an educational degree, a successful farm or business or whatever. But what such a claim fails to observe is the web of interdependence which made the accomplishment possible. Instead, we attribute the achievement to our own ambition and prowess. Unfortunately this attitude leads to the claim that anybody, if they simply applied themselves, could accomplish the same thing. By emphasizing the individual character of the achievement, we ignore the web of interdependence which so often *prevents* others from "making it," such as poor schools, "wrong" color of skin, bad nutrition, or low expectations from peer groups. Instead, we create misleading myths about those who haven't "made it": that their dispossessed position is caused by their laziness, lack of ambition, lack of cleanliness, or even by their genetic intellectual inferiority. One of the most necessary ingredients for an understanding of the need for *social* change (as opposed to simply changing individuals) is this perception that we live in a web of interdependence, a perception that is dulled or eradicated by our individualistic creed.

A third obstacle to understanding radical social change is the common "model" or "image" that most of us unconsciously use in thinking about society. Most of us tend to operate with a "good-better" image of the way in which society should change. Society, according to this view, is basically healthy; what is needed is modest correction and adjustment so that the good can evolve into the better. Such betterment will occur through the democratic process, through channels — and what is more sacred than the democratic process? This image of change is quite appropriate in some situations; but if applied to all situations, it clearly limits our vision or perception of what might be possible in some situations. It rules out the possibility that something significant and healthy might be occurring outside of structures; and it prevents us from perceiving that there are situations which call for a total rebuilding rather than a continued construction on foundations that, though once healthy, may have rotted.

A fourth "cultural" reason for not striving to understand social change is that many consider the advocates of social change "uncouth." While there are many clean-cut, middle-aged, and elderly advocates of social change, the mental image that the words "change" and "conflict" suggest to many is that of a young, bearded, possibly black, unconventionally dressed, arrogant individual. There is the abrasiveness of their language when they indict "whitey" or "the establishment" or anybody over thirty. There is their seeming rejection of so much that we accept as normal in their experimentation with drugs, changing sexual mores, Afro haircuts on black radicals, and repudiation of middle class economic values. Then there is the use of unconventional tactics: interrupting church services, burning draft cards, confronting police, and occupying buildings. If being committed to social change means to "get into that bag," many American Christians, rightly or wrongly, are likely to hesitate.

A final manifestation of our failure to grapple with change and conflict is that many scholars committed to the scientific study of society have devoted relatively little attention to social conflict, especially in textbooks, and have failed to develop a theory of social conflict. To the credit of sociology, it is from within that discipline itself that a small number of sociologists have made this self-criticism.[10] Their research models show a marked preference for stability and equilibrium; conflict is often described in terms which, though analytical, have a decidedly negative connotation: "pathology," "deviant behavior." The reasons suggested for this negative attitude toward conflict, or its neglect, are manifold: many sociologists reflect their culture's distaste for conflict; textbooks need a wide acceptance to be produced and thus cannot deal with "unpopular" subjects sympathetically or at length; most scientific study of society in the United States is sponsored by institutions that have a stake in the preservation of the present order (foundations, universities, government grants).[11] This is not only a barrier to understanding — i.e., we don't have as much scientific groundwork as we could use — it is yet another demonstration of our endemic distaste for change and conflict.

THE REAL OBSTACLE?

Although the preceding list of religious and cultural barriers to understanding social change may give the impression that there is a multiplicity of independent causes that stand in the way, they are probably not independent causes, but manifestations or rationalizations of a far more profound barrier to social change in our ethos: most of us, the readers of this book and the author, are really quite well-treated by the present structures, at least superficially. Life for us is secure, affluent, beneficent. We may occasionally agonize about the problems of those against whom rampant injustice is committed, but we have the luxury of being able to ignore those problems whenever we wish to (or at least we think we can), as a black American, or a Vietnamese, or a parent of a starving child in the developing nations cannot. We can imagine much worse societies for ourselves; but we cannot imagine much better ones. As a result any significant change seems threatening, for the outcome of such change is unpredictable.

If we conceive of our self-interest in quite *narrow* terms (the well-being of ourselves, our families and the small group of acquaintances that we know well), then we will likely conclude that it is in our self-interest to maintain, or at most slightly modify, the present social and political arrangement. Rather than admit that we really want to preserve the status quo, we rationalize it by finding "good reasons," whether they be an otherworldly conception of the Christian faith, separation of religion and politics, or the "uncouthness" of the radicals.

This two-sided phenomenon—our satisfaction with the way things are and our fear of what change might do to our status — is very well-expressed in the following statement:

> Our political and social institutions also resist change. Many are too happy to accept their comfortable heritage and too unwilling to respond to the proper demands of their brother men. Many of us, perhaps all, fear change; we fear to be disturbed and to lose what we often possess unrighteously at the expense of others. More deeply we fear the uncertainty of change,

23

the unknown future and the unpredictability of cir-cumstances.[12]

That most or all of the barriers to understanding social change and conflict are in fact manifestations or rationalizations of our self-interest in preserving the status quo may seem like a harsh judgment. The rest of this book will give one an opportunity to make his own judgment about the validity or invalidity of these barriers; that is, to make a judgment as to whether those barriers are authentically grounded in scripture and human experience, or whether they are our self-serving inventions.

AMOS: A CASE STUDY

3

After indicating the massive prominence of social change and the barriers which need to be overcome to understand its relationship to Christian faithfulness, it is illuminating to turn to a figure in the biblical tradition: the eighth century B.C. prophet Amos.[1]

Amos' background was humble. He tells us that he was a shepherd in the arid uplands of Tekoa and a dresser of sycamore trees (1:1, 7:14-15). Not only are these seasonal occupations, but the sheep of Tekoa produced only the coarsest wool, and the fruit of the sycamore tree was a very poor fruit, eaten only by the poorest of people. So Amos was a seasonal worker, working in two marginal occupations. In contemporary terms, he could be described as a migrant worker. He is very clear that he is not an official religious worker (7:14); he was, in fact, a layman, having no professional status.

But this will not be a rags-to-riches story of a man of

humble origins who turned into a successful and re-
spected citizen, like Abraham Lincoln or Horatio Alger.
For Amos never attained respectability; there is little
chance that he was thought of as anything other than a
rabble-rousing crank during his lifetime. Indeed, he does
sound like a rabble-rouser; in words as sharp as a well-
honed machete, he savagely indicted the society of his
day, a society characterized by deep divisions between
the well-to-do and the poor. Moreover, he had the
audacity to affirm that these words were the Word of
God. Little comfort or hope is found in the written
record of his words; the semi-hopeful concluding verses
of chapter nine are viewed by virtually all scholars as an
addition by a later editor who wanted the book to have
a happier ending. (Even these verses are not too com-
forting; they speak of "restoration," which logically requires a preceding period of destruction and chaos.)

What did Amos say to his society, to the "church" of
his day? [2] As we attack this question, it may be most
helpful to place ourselves, not in the prophet's shoes, but
in the shoes of the people whom he addressed. Then we
can appreciate what he said much more clearly.

Perhaps the most useful way to introduce Amos is to
refer to his "inaugural speech" (1:3–2:16), and, by using
one's historical imagination, to set that speech in its
probable context. It is likely that these words were spoken by Amos at the autumn festival at the chief shrine to
God in the northern kingdom. This festival was a day
of both religious and patriotic significance; it was the
day that Israel celebrated that the Lord was her god; it
was a day when Israel hoped that God would vindicate
her against her enemies, the neighboring states. One can
imagine thousands of church members flocked together
in the predawn darkness at Bethel, waiting for the festival
to begin. As the sun rises, Amos begins to speak (undoubtedly, he was *not* on the program of official speak-
ers):

> Thus says the Lord:
> For three transgressions of Damascus,
> and for four, I will not revoke the punishment (1:3).

26

The crowd probably has its interest whetted by this statement: here's a chap, claiming to speak in the name of God, who says that Damascus, that ancient enemy of the church (Israel), is going to get it in the neck! Amos continues:

> Thus says the Lord:
> For three transgressions of Gaza,
> and for four, I will not revoke the punishment (1:6).

The crowd stirs; another enemy of the church is going to be destroyed! And then, in rapid succession, using the same highly rhythmic, somber phraseology, Amos denounces Tyre, Edom, Amon, Moab, and Judah (Judah was a military enemy of Israel, the northern kingdom, at this time). By this time the crowd has undoubtedly reached a frenzy of enthusiasm: "Go get 'em, Amos, tell it like it is — all of the enemies of Israel are going to be destroyed by God!" And that's what God is for, isn't it? To protect his church, the faithful?

But Amos has not finished. He has one more stanza to add:

> Thus says the Lord:
> For three transgressions of Israel
> and for four, I will not revoke the punishment (2:6).

The crowd suddenly becomes hushed; and then probably erupts into a howl of frenzy. God punishing Israel, the church? Who does this vagabond migrant think he is, anyway?

But the harsh invective of Amos is not exhausted by the brilliantly systematic inaugural speech. Listen to a few more of his words:

> Hear this word, you cows of Bashan,
> who are in the mountain of Samaria,
> who oppress the poor, who crush the needy,
> who say to their husbands,
> "Bring, that we may drink!"
> The Lord God has sworn by his holiness
> that, behold, the days are coming upon you,
> when they shall take you away with hooks,
> even the last of you with fishhooks (4:1-2).

Here is this man, who dares to call the ladies of Samaria (the ladies' aid) "cows of Bashan"! And he tells these fine people that they will be carried away by hooks. How intemperate and uncouth can one get?

About the religious ceremonies of Israel, which were apparently quite orthodox and dedicated to God, Amos says, in the name of God:

> I hate, I despise your feasts [religious feasts — dare we say pot-luck suppers?]
> and I take no delight in your solemn assemblies.
> Even though you offer me your burnt offerings and cereal offerings [the prescribed method of worship; i.e., they used the right liturgy],
> I will not accept them,
> and the peace offerings of your fatted beasts
> I will not look upon.
> Take away from me the noise of your hymns;
> to the melody of your harps [organs] I will not listen.
> But let justice roll down like waters,
> and righteousness like an everflowing stream
> (5:21-24; see also 4:4-5; 5:4-5; 9:7).

Doesn't Amos hold anything sacred? Surely God longs for our worship. What do you mean, Amos, by saying that God hates our religious services? Surely you are wrong!

As one would expect, the senior priest at Bethel, Amaziah, reacts quite strongly to this: "O seer [an insulting term], go, flee away to the land of Judah . . . , but never again prophesy at Bethel!" (7:12-13). Amaziah also sends a message to the king that this rabble-rouser is speaking treason (7:10). How does Amos respond to Amaziah's order to get out? He says, "Go tell the king that his country will be destroyed, that the princes will be killed, and that his wife will be a whore in the inner city" (7:17). Good old diplomatic Amos!

So, initially, Amos tells Israel that she is going to be destroyed, that the structures of church and state will collapse, and that it is the will of the force which drives history, the will of God, that this happen. It is critical to note, moreover, that Amos is not speaking of the end of the world; the impending collapse is clearly an event *within history*, an invasion by a foreign power (see, e.g.,

1:14-15, 2:2-3, 3:11, 6:14). Hence Amos is not a seer of the distant end-time; instead, he speaks of contemporary history in Israel, and seeks to interpret the meaning of that history.

But why this wrath? Why this immoderate excitement? What is it about that society that kindles the wrath of God, according to Amos? Two groupings of indictments provide the answer. In the first place, God is horrified by the barbarities of warfare, about atrocities committed against civilians: "You have threshed [the people of] Gilead with threshing sledges of iron; they have ripped up women with child in Gilead; they delivered a whole people to Edom [to be slaves]" (1:3, 1:9, 1:13). The shrieks of Amos are really verbal atrocity posters.

But the bulk of the book is devoted to the second grouping of indictments where Amos speaks of God's wrath because of the oppressive conditions of urban Israel: poverty, unfair treatment of the poor in the courts, lack of compassion toward the oppressed. But listen to Amos' own words.

To the women he says:

> *Hear this word, you cows of Bashan . . .*
> *who oppress the poor, who crush the needy . . .(4:1).*

Of Israel as a whole he says:

> *They sell the righteous for silver and*
> *the needy for a pair of shoes — they trample*
> *the head of the poor into the dust of the earth,*
> *and turn aside the way of the afflicted (2:6-7).*

Amos (and God for whom he speaks) is shocked at economic conditions that permit such poverty, especially in the midst of plenty, as the next indictment makes clear:

> *Woe to those who lie upon beds of ivory,*
> *and stretch themselves upon their couches,*
> *and eat lambs from the flock,*
> *and calves from the midst of the stall;*
> *who sing idle songs to the sound of the harp,*
> *and like David invent for themselves instruments*
> *of music;*

29

> who drink wine in bowls,
> and anoint themselves with the finest oils,
> but are not grieved over the ruin of Joseph! (6:4-6).

Is Amos really against such activities as eating good food, singing, drinking, and inventing musical instruments? Or is he saying that it is scandalous that people can be oblivious to the fate of the poor ("the ruin of Joseph"), carrying on business and leisure as usual? Either alternative is devastating.

In other words, Amos is claiming that Israel will collapse at the will of God because of the glaring inequities of her social and economic life.

What then does this ruffian want from Israel? Does he want them to be more pious, to be more faithful in their tithing? No, they already know how to do that very well, perhaps too well (4:4-5). What then? Again, let Amos speak:

> Seek good, and not evil,
> that you may live . . .
> Hate evil, and love good,
> and establish justice in the gate (5:14-15).

> Let justice roll down like waters,
> and righteousness like an everflowing stream (5:24).

And, besides explicit passages such as the above, it is easy to discern from Amos' negative statements what he expected from Israel (the church): justice. And he founds this exhortation for justice in God's gracious act to Israel at the Exodus. In 2:10-11, he says, in effect: Remember who you are, Israel; that you were slaves in Egypt, oppressed, and that I brought you out of there; therefore, do not be oppressors now! Remember who you are.

It is important to note that justice for Amos is not a "spiritual" word in the popular sense of the term "spiritual." It is a word that relates to the marketplace, to economics, to politics. Nor is it charity. Amos is not saying, "Remember the poor at Christmas time with a food-basket" (not that that's bad). No, for Amos justice has to do with the structures of the society.

Now that we have distilled the positive content of the

message of Amos to the phrase "seek justice" we must immediately insist that the phrase be expanded once again. For men differ on what constitutes justice, and what one man calls good, another man calls bad. But for Amos, justice means a particular kind of concern:

> [the prophets] would never have been willing to abstract such statements [like "seek justice"] from their contexts. They will not have their message reduced to platitudes or moral generalizations. . . . Prophetic ethics is most itself when it is most concrete, indeed when it is most offensive to those who appeal to generalizations to be good. When Amos cries out, "Seek good and not evil that you may live," the context makes it clear exactly what he means. It means establishing justice in the gate, where the poor were being deprived of their rights. It means to "seek the Lord and live," to bring into effect and to implement the basic rights which belong to every man in the community. The prophets keep calling for justice, justice for every man, and especially for those most liable to be treated unjustly . . . because they speak for the God of justice and compassion who intervenes in behalf of the exploited and weak and defenseless.[3]

Hence the focus of Amos' concern is clearly upon the oppressed.

What are we to do with Amos? Quite frankly, it's not comfortable to be well-acquainted with Amos; it would be much more comfortable to have religion be concerned with something else. It is difficult to preach from Amos, for he seems to suggest that much of what we do in church is really not that important. If we feel this discomfort, then perhaps we have succeeded in placing ourselves at least partially in the shoes of his hearers. But, whatever we finally make of Amos, there are several important insights that emerge from the words of this stranger, whom our fathers (God bless them) canonized.

1. Amos is convinced that the Word of God is profoundly concerned with this-worldly affairs. There is no separation of religion and politics here: indeed, it is Amaziah, the villain of this story, who would have been happy to make such a separation!

2. Confronted with social conflict between the have's and the have-not's in Israel, Amos interprets it as a call for judgment from a righteous God — and it is a this-worldly judgment. The Word of God interprets the meaning of conflict and chaos.

3. By our standards, Amos is undoubtedly uncouth; he is irrevocably negative, unconscionably blunt, terrifyingly harsh. Not only that, but he had no official right to speak; instead, as he puts it, God "took me from following the flock," i.e., he spoke from an inner compulsion that God's word needed to be heard. He had no credentials that the people could recognize; there was no way that they could discern that he was a genuine prophet, and perhaps even Amos himself at times doubted it.

4. Finally, and very crucially, Amos affirms that the radical social change about which he speaks (the coming collapse of the structures) will be brought about by God. The old structures are so filled with injustice and sin and unresponsiveness that probably only a new beginning on the other side of chaos can have a chance of being more just. In short, God is active in radical social change, and his faithful follower is called to respond to that action—to seek justice.

It hardly needs to be said that an acquaintance with Amos demolishes in principle the barriers to understanding social change that were delineated in chapter two. That is, it is not that being acquainted with Amos suddenly makes it easy to understand social change; but what it does do is to make emphatically clear that a person who stands in the tradition of Amos must seek to relate his faithfulness to God to the public order.

But the question still remains, what do we do with Amos? How do we relate his searing passion for justice to our time, and to the church? Or is it even necessary to do that? Perhaps, after all, he is a minority of one in the biblical tradition. Later in this book we shall have to investigate that question and set Amos within a broader biblical-theological framework.

THE MONTGOMERY STORY: A CONTEMPORARY CASE STUDY

4

To a large extent, the first three chapters have had a very limited though critically important purpose: to demonstrate the magnitude of social change and conflict, and to suggest that the biblical figure of Amos gives us a mandate to understand and direct social change, despite the formidable barriers outlined in chapter two. In this and succeeding chapters, we must move to a more detailed analysis of conflict as an element of social change.

CASE STUDY: THE MONTGOMERY STORY

On December 1, 1955, Mrs. Rosa Parks, a black seamstress, was on her way home from work on a segregated city bus in Montgomery, Alabama. Although properly seated in the back of the bus, she was asked to give up her seat to a white man who had just boarded. Weary

33

from being on her feet most of the day, she refused, since giving up her seat would have meant standing in the now-full bus. She was promptly arrested and taken to jail, for it was illegal for a black person to refuse to give up her seat to a white. Her arrest sparked off a movement with immediate effects on Montgomery and long-range effects on the entire nation, including the emergence of Martin Luther King as a national leader.[1] We shall analyze this episode both because it is an important chapter in contemporary history and because it provides us with a useful tool for raising certain crucial questions about conflict and social change.

To appreciate this incident fully, one has to set it in its broader context. Of the 50,000 black people in Montgomery, 17,500 used the buses twice daily to commute to work and school. Indeed black people constituted 75 percent of the riders on the buses. Yet despite the overwhelming financial dependence of the bus company on black commuters, certain insulting practices prevailed:

> The seating arrangement: Blacks were required to sit in the back; a section in front was reserved for whites. Between the two sections was "neutral" ground; but if a black person sat here, he or she could legally be required to give up the seat to a white person.

> The discourteousness of the bus drivers: On many occasions, the drivers openly referred to black people as "niggers," "black cows," "black apes."

> Boarding procedures: Frequently a bus driver would require a black person to pay his fare at the front of the bus, and then get off the bus to walk around to the back doors to board. Not only was this an inconvenience, but occasionally the driver would deliberately drive off before the black person could make it around to the back doors.

> Hiring procedures: Despite the fact that 75 percent of the riders were black, it was company policy not to hire black drivers.

Besides these regular practices, there were several incidents preceding Mrs. Parks' arrest. On one occasion a

15 year-old black girl refused to give up her seat to a white, was arrested, handcuffed, and convicted. Following this the black community threatened a boycott and received a promise from the bus manager and police commissioner that more courteous treatment would prevail in the future. The promise was not fulfilled. On another occasion a black man boarded a crowded bus, paid his fare, and was told by the driver to get off and board through the back doors. Looking toward the back of the bus, the man saw that it would be impossible to board from the back, so he asked for his dime back. The driver refused, the police were called, and the man was shot and killed after an argument and scuffle. It was, of course, an "accident" and "nobody's fault."

But these dramatic incidents must be read cautiously, for they tend to overshadow what was really at stake in the bus company's policy: the day-to-day psychological consequences of being treated as an inferior. As social psychologists have demonstrated, the effect of discriminatory treatment upon the discriminated is to make them believe that they actually are inferior.

But even the bus system as a whole is only symptomatic of a larger system which prevailed in Montgomery, many elements of which still persist today, in both North and South. Black people were excluded from most occupations except manual and domestic work and those professional occupations which served black people (morticians, clergy, doctors). Furthermore, the median annual income for white people was double that of black people, which can be accounted for only in terms of unjust social structures, unless one believes in genetic white superiority. There was, of course, the segregated school system, as well as segregation in transportation, recreation, restaurants, and hotels. Finally, there were the barriers placed in front of black voters. Of 30,000 black people of voting age in Montgomery County, only 2000 were registered, because of discriminatory registration procedures. Hence one of the few means of "using the channels"—the ballot—was effectively denied.

In fairness to the white people of Montgomery, it should be observed that black people may have given the impression that they liked the system, because of their passive outward acceptance of these conditions. Such passivity, Dr. King notes, has "sometimes given our white brothers the feeling that we liked the way we were being treated."[2] Both black and white accepted the system as a matter of course, so firmly ingrained was it.

After the arrest of Mrs. Parks several clergymen, including Dr. King, then a young 27 year-old pastor, called together a group of black leaders to decide what was to be done. They decided on a one day boycott of the buses for the following Monday, December 5. The immense task of communicating this decision to the black community was accomplished partly through announcements in church on Sunday, partly through mimeographed leaflets, and partly through a newspaper article attacking the impending action. Had it not been for the hostile article, thousands of black people would probably not have learned of the boycott.

The leaders hoped for 60 percent success. King and his wife arose at 5:30 a.m. on Monday to watch the first buses go by their home; the first three buses carried a total of two white people and no black people, and normally these buses would have been filled to capacity with black workers! Rather than 60 percent, the boycott on Monday was over 99 percent successful! That night a mass meeting of thousands of black people was held at a large black church to decide whether to continue the boycott. Some leaders thought it should be continued in order to bring more pressure to bear on the city commission and the bus company; others thought it should stop while it was still a success, rather than risking a gradual dwindling in the next few days. After all, could they really expect 17,500 regular riders to find alternative means of transportation, or to walk? The meeting included singing, prayers, devotions, a sermon by Dr. King, and a vote—a unanimous vote to continue the boycott.

The immediate problem was to organize alternative means of transportation and to form a representative group to negotiate. In response to this, the Montgomery Improvement Association was formed with Dr. King as president. Two alternative means of transportation were devised. The eighteen black taxi companies of Montgomery agreed to have their 210 taxis provide rides to black people for the same price as a bus ride. A volunteer car pool was also organized, later supplemented by 15 station wagons purchased with contributions that began to flow in from all over the world. Even though these alternative means were available, many black people preferred to walk, some as many as twelve miles a day.

Three demands were formulated by the MIA: 1) The bus company should take steps to insure courteous treatment by bus drivers; 2) Seating should be on a first-come, first-served basis, with black people seated from the back forward and white people seated from the front backward; 3) When vacancies occurred, black drivers should be hired for buses serving primarily black routes. Several meetings occurred in December between the MIA and the city commission and bus company. The city offered to encourage the drivers to be courteous, but would not alter either the seating arrangements or the hiring practices. The boycott continued.

During the course of the boycott, a variety of methods of resistance were used by whites in Montgomery—some official, some quite unofficial and illegal. On December 8, three days after the boycott began, the city announced that it would enforce a law calling for a minimum cab fare of 45 cents, thus eliminating the black taxis as a replacement form of transportation. The black community responded by expanding the previously-mentioned car pool and later purchasing 15 station wagons. (Incidentally, each wagon carried the name of a church on it, so the black churches were closely identified with the movement—indeed, passengers could often be heard singing hymns as the wagons passed.)

The MIA was also harassed in its attempt to secure regular meeting rooms and office space. Originally they met in the Alabama Negro Baptist Center, but white officials of the Baptist church threatened to withdraw financial support for the Center, and so the MIA was forced to move to a black-owned "Citizens Club," normally used for banquets. The city threatened to take away its food and beverage licenses, because it was being used as an office building. Again the MIA moved, this time to a black church impervious to white financial pressures.

Next, the MIA was told during the negotiations that the proposed seating regulations would violate the city's law. Actually, it was questionable whether it would have, and change of the law would not have been difficult.

Dr. King's leadership was attacked by the city negotiating group, and it was strongly implied that he was the major barrier to successful resolution of the conflict. Other attempts were made to discredit his leadership and divide the black community. It was said that the leaders were only interested in money; that it was too bad for the older black clergy that they had had their rightful place of leadership taken by one so young. This campaign actually led Dr. King to offer his resignation to the MIA; it was unanimously refused.

Perhaps the most striking attempt of the city to divide and confuse the black community came on January 22, seven weeks into the boycott. The city announced in the newspaper that a settlement had been reached with three prominent representative black clergymen, and that black people should resume riding the buses. In fact, the three clergymen were neither prominent nor representative, nor had they agreed to the city's offer!

Also in January, the three city commissioners announced that they had joined the White Citizens Council, a "respectable" group committed to segregation and white supremacy. The police also began to harass and arrest car-pool drivers, as well as informing black people who were walking or waiting for rides that they were in danger of violating ordinances against hitchhiking and vagrancy. King himself was arrested for speeding—allegedly 30 miles per hour in a 25 miles per hour zone. He was taken to jail.

Threatening cards, letters and calls reached Dr. King at the rate of 30 to 40 per day. On January 30, the threats became incarnate when his home was bombed while he was speaking at a rally. Though his wife and child were at home, they were not injured. Later in the campaign the homes of other black leaders and black churches were bombed. Nobody was ever convicted for these bombings, even though some white people signed confessions to the latter bombings. They were acquitted.

In February, an anti-boycott law was found which prohibited boycotting in an unjust or illegal cause. Warrants for the arrest of over 100 black people were issued, and about 90, including King, were actually brought to trial. King was found guilty and sentenced to a $500 fine or 386 days at hard labor.

In September the 15 station wagons operated by the MIA began to have difficulty keeping their liability insurance, as insurance companies repeatedly cancelled their policies. This was resolved by insuring them with Lloyd's of London.

Finally, on October 30, after nearly eleven months of boycott, the city made a move which seemed likely to break the ability of the black community to continue the struggle. It announced a hearing to determine whether the MIA car pool was a private enterprise operating without a franchise (if so, it would be illegal), or whether the car pool was a voluntary, non-profit, "share-a-ride" operation (then it would be legal). The hearing was convened on November 13, and few black people had any illusions as to what the decision would be.

But on that same day while court was in session, word was received from Washington, D.C., that the U.S. Supreme Court had upheld a lower court decision that segregated buses were contrary to the 14th Amendment. The initial suit had been initiated by the MIA, and its successful resolution meant that they had won. But still it was not possible for the black people of Montgomery to resume riding the buses, for the city refused to integrate them until the actual written order arrived from Washington. This did not occur for another five weeks, on December 20; on December 21, the black people of Montgomery began riding again. For over twelve months, they had walked, shared rides, sung, prayed, met, cried, and shared an experience that shaped black-white relationships for many years hence.

Clearly this situation could not have been resolved without conflict, which we shall now define in a preliminary way as the attempt to bend another person or group to one's will and the resistance offered to such an attempt. That change could not have occurred without conflict is amply demonstrated by the manifold attempts of most of the white community to prevent change. It is unlikely that education or articulate persuasion would have accomplished the change when it took the combined force of an economic boycott and the federal courts over twelve months to resolve the issue. Thus we have a vivid example of conflict as an inevitable accompaniment to this particular social change.

But there is far more to be learned from this episode than the simple—but important—observation that conflict was a necessary part of it. For King was operating with a specific strategy of social change that needs to be examined to further our understanding of conflict and social change.

King described his strategy as "non-violent resistance." Founded, according to King, on the *agape* love of Jesus and the teachings of Gandhi, its basic premise is withdrawal of cooperation from an evil system. King, following Thoreau, argued that he who passively accepts an evil system is guilty of perpetuating it. That is, to do nothing against an unjust status quo is to insure its continued existence.

In addition to this basic premise, there are six ingredients to non-violent resistance as formulated by King:

> *1. One is actively resistant to evil, though only in a non-violent way. Thus it is not passive non-resistance, but active non-violent resistance.*
>
> *2. One seeks to create a feeling of shame in the opponent, and thus to lead him to repentance and reconciliation. That is, it is an appeal to his conscience.*
>
> *3. One attacks an evil system rather than persons.*
>
> *4. One willingly accepts violence, imprisonment, or whatever else the oppressor attempts, but one will not inflict violence.*
>
> *5. One seeks to act always out of love so as not to increase hostility, and conversely, to increase the possibility of binding up the broken community.*
>
> *6. One must have a faith that the power behind the universe is on the side of love and justice, even when all the evidence may suggest the contrary. Otherwise one will not be able to persevere.*

Thus King's understanding of the successful outcome of the Montgomery story is that it was a triumph for *agape* love operating through non-violent resistance. It was, according to King, a successful appeal to the conscience of man. King himself sums up his strategy in the following words:

> Here non-violence comes in as the ultimate form of persuasion. It is the method which seeks to implement the just law by appealing to the conscience of the great decent majority who through blindness, fear, pride, and irrationality have allowed their consciences to sleep.[3]

The italicized words are the critical ones. King himself understands his actions as *persuasion, appealing to the conscience of the majority.*

If persuasion and appeals to conscience can bring about social change, the role of conflict can perhaps be minimized. But did non-violence as understood by King really win the day in Montgomery? To be sure, it clearly affected many responses, and in a beneficial way. For example, after King's house was bombed, an angry group of black people gathered around the wreckage, ready to wreak revenge on white people. In an impassioned speech, King appealed to them in the name of Jesus:

> If you have weapons, take them home; if you do not have them, please do not seek to get them. We cannot solve this problem through retaliatory violence. We must meet violence with nonviolence. Remember the words of Jesus: "He who lives by the sword will perish by the sword."[4]

The crowd went home. Indeed, the restraint of the black community during the entire protest is remarkable and certainly attributable to King's leadership. Before black people resumed riding the buses, the MIA carefully instructed them to avoid being arrogant, to avoid gloating about their success, to respond non-violently and in a friendly way if physically attacked or verbally insulted by whites, to travel in pairs so that each might strengthen the other's non-violence. As a result, the eventual integration of the buses went admirably well, except

41

for actions from terrorist elements in the white community. But black people did not respond in kind. Clearly, then, King's non-violence minimized bloodshed. But the question still remains: is it correct to understand it as persuasion, as King did?

An equally convincing case could be made that it was *power* that won the day, not appeals to conscience through persuasion. In economic terms, the boycott was costly to both the city and the bus company. The city was entitled to two percent of bus revenue, and the city's loss was $15,000; hence the bus company's loss was around $750,000. There was also the weight of negative public opinion in much of the nation, which obviously pleased neither the Chamber of Commerce nor the business community. Finally, it was a federal court ruling, with the implied power of the federal government to enforce it, that ultimately caused the city to capitulate. Hence the question remains: was the city persuaded or coerced into settlement? Or, to put it differently, is appeal to conscience through moral argument an efficacious way of social change? Or is the use of power (which can, of course, be nonviolent) necessary? To this question we must turn in the next chapter.

There is also a second matter that requires our attention. How did conflict function in the Montgomery story? That is, was it wholly destructive (as it seems in the bombings) or was there also a creative side to it? To this question we must turn in chapter seven.

STRATEGIES OF SOCIAL CHANGE

5

After the case study of Dr. King in Montgomery, it becomes imperative to raise in a general manner the question with which the last chapter ended. How is justice to be achieved? That is, how are significant changes in the structures of society to be brought about? In short, how is social change to be achieved?

In our contemporary culture there are at least three different approaches to achieving social change: the individualistic approach, the consensus approach, and the coercive or conflict approach.

THE INDIVIDUALISTIC APPROACH TO SOCIAL CHANGE

The best way to bring about social change, according to this view, is to change the attitudes of individual men or, if you please, to change their hearts. Such individual attitudinal change will then produce a change in the individual's behavior. This view is quite common in our folk wisdom; one hears it said, "No law or change in law can produce love in my heart for another man"; hence structural changes are downgraded. The solution to the race problem, to use a concrete issue, is to change individual attitudes so that black men and white men will freely love each other, and this will insure just, loving behavior. How such attitudinal change is brought about can be described in religious terms as "conversion" and in non-religious terms as education or persuasion.

THE CONSENSUS APPROACH TO SOCIAL CHANGE

This is similar to the first approach since it assumes that persuasion and education can bring about social change, but it differs in that it affirms the importance of legislation and other similar structural changes. It is assumed that if a problem is demonstrably a serious one involving obvious injustice, the democratic process will respond to the "consensus" opinion. Above all, the route to change is through channels: through elected representatives, the courts, agencies of local, state, and federal government. According to this approach society is essentially harmonious and stable, and change not only ought to be but can be achieved in an *orderly* manner.

This view operates with a certain view of the American past: that the American way of doing things is through the democratic process, and that this has worked admirably well in achieving the society that we have today. More drastic methods of change may be justified in other countries where legitimate channels of change are not available, but not here.

THE COERCIVE OR CONFLICT APPROACH

According to this approach significant social change occurs in a society most commonly—perhaps only—in a time of conflict or crisis. It does not abdicate the democratic process, but argues that the democratic process does not respond except to crises; that there is a reciprocal relationship between the democratic process and conflict. Hence, change almost always is produced by conflict. Such conflict can be accidentally produced —as in the case of the Great Depression—or it can be deliberately produced. It is in the case of deliberately produced conflict that the term "coercion," the use of power, has its meaning. Here it is argued that social change comes about through the use of power—not necessarily sufficient power to impose one's will on the rest of society, but sufficient power to create a conflict that cannot be ignored. (It should be noted that "power" and "violence" are not synonymous terms in this context.)

Which of these competing strategies for bringing about social change is most correct? How does one go about answering such a question? Simply in terms of personal preferences—i.e., "I like model one better"—or is there a more objective way of arriving at an answer? Two relatively objective criteria will be employed to attempt an answer: the evidence of history, and the nature of man.

THE EVIDENCE OF HISTORY

Approaches one and two both depend upon the success of persuasion—in the first approach, upon persuasion of individuals, and upon the persuasion of a majority in the second. Does American history offer impressive evidence for the validity of the persuasive approach? Does it show that change has occurred through orderly, democratic means, or through the conversion of individuals?

We can begin by noting that the birth, continued union, and expansion of the United States all were accomplished through conflict, and through the most virulent form of conflict: war. In addition, most of the major changes in legislation and social policies have not been brought about through a consensus arrived at by persuasion, but in response to conflict and crisis. Some examples should suffice to make this point clear.

The rise of the labor movement was accompanied by strikes, boycotts, and occasional overt violence. The movement for women suffrage created conflict at almost every stage. The rise of most immigrant groups involved conflict and power-struggles. The abolition of slavery was not accomplished except by war. One contemporary historian observes that the history of the United States has been characterized by outbreaks of violence in every generation, and then cites eleven examples to document his case. He concludes:

> Whoever supposes, then, that American politics has been nothing more than a moving consensus, a sort of national Rotary Club luncheon, has not sufficiently reflected on the regularity of intense conflict, crisis, and violence in American history.[1]

This is not meant to be a cynical view of the American experience, nor is it meant to debunk that experience, nor is it meant to glorify conflict and violence. It is intended to paint a more realistic picture of the way in which change occurs as opposed to the misleading notion that the American way has always been one of orderly change. Instead, substantial changes in the structures of American institutions have normally occurred as a response to conflict. To cite more general examples: the mass of new social legislation in the 1930s came as a response to the crisis of the Great Depression; the emergence of the United States as a nation with worldwide concerns after World War II occurred as a response to the power vacuum created by World War II and the existence of Russia as a new world power; the cluster of civil right acts in 1964-68 occurred not because we had suddenly decided that it would be a good idea, but as a response to the conflicts and crises engendered by the civil rights movement. This brief survey would seem to point to the validity of the coercive or conflict approach: structures change not through education or persuasion, but through responses to crisis, conflict, and power.

THE NATURE OF MAN

Second, and here we shall find the theological tradition of immense assistance, each approach to understanding social change presupposes different understandings of the nature of man.

46

Models one and two assume that man is essentially reasonable, and that once he can be shown the injustices present in a situation, he will seek to rectify them. Basically, we are men of good-will, at least the educated among us. To be sure, there are criminals and deranged people ("the lunatic fringe") in our midst, but most of us can be counted on to do the right thing, once we know what it is. Hence the problem is ignorance, and the solution is education. This attitude is manifest in statements such as, "If we could only come to realize that we're all alike under the skin, then our problems would be solved." It is also a widespread notion among social scientists:

> By mid-century sociologists and psychologists, although formally eschewing the role of the social engineer, had come to a position of implicit faith in the intrinsic harmony of social systems and the natural reasonableness of the individual.[2]

Model three, however, assumes a quite different understanding of human nature. It assumes that man acts essentially out of self-interest, that he will respond otherwise only when a crisis has become unbearable, or when sufficient power or coercion is exerted upon him to make it in his self-interest to change. Which of these two views of human nature is most correct and, by implication, which model of social change is most likely to be effective?

One could simply answer the question about human nature in a sentence. However, it may be more instructive to arrive at an answer inductively by referring to concrete incidents in a case study.

During World War II civilian citizens of the Allied nations in China were placed in internment camps for the duration of the war. The following vignettes are taken from the experience of one of those camps, documented by Langdon Gilkey in his book *Shantung Compound*.[3]

Originally, about 2200 civilians found themselves interred in the camp in which Gilkey found himself. These people were mostly well-educated professional people: Americans, British, Belgians; doctors, lawyers, teachers, missionaries, businessmen, a cross-section of the middle class. Conditions at the camp were grim, but beatings, torture, and extermination were not used as in many con-centration camps in Europe. Instead, on the grounds of a former missionary compound, these people carved out for themselves a functioning community, subject of course to the Japanese authorities.

Gilkey entered the camp with a fairly high estimate of the human capacity to live together. His estimate was initially confirmed by the first experiences of camp life. The internees showed great inventiveness and ingenuity in creating liveable quarters, in operating the kitchens and latrines, in the technical activities of creating a com-munity.

But in a very short time, a quite different picture began to emerge. Gilkey was head of the camp housing com-mittee, charged with securing fair housing for internees and with hearing complaints. Housing was, of course, cramped. One day representatives of one room came to Gilkey, pointing out that they had eleven men in their room, and that the room across the hall had only nine. Obviously, since the rooms were exactly the same size, the just course of action was to move one man from the room with eleven to the room with nine. Gilkey agreed to present their case to the nine men, and he describes his attitude as he went to the room:

> *"Are not people rational and moral?" I asked myself. "Does this not mean — if it means anything — that the average man, when faced with a clear case of in-justice which his mind can distinctly perceive, will at the least agree to rectify that injustice — even if he himself suffers from that rectification?"* [4]

The nine men responded in a quite different manner: we're already crowded enough, it's no concern of ours, and get out or we'll throw you out. That is, it was in their self-interest not to give up a few inches of space each, and so justice lost. As Gilkey comments, "Self-interest seemed almost omnipotent next to the weak claims of logic and fair play."[5] The situation was rec-tified only by introducing Japanese power. The point: power, not persuasion, achieved a more just arrangement.

The housing of families provides us with a second

example. When the internees first moved in, the Japanese gave two rooms (nine feet by twelve feet) to each of the families with two teen-aged children, and one room (also nine by twelve) to the families with two younger children or infants. This soon became intolerable, for the younger children had to stay indoors during the cold damp winter. (Any parent can appreciate the chaos in such a situation.) On the other hand, the teenagers were more often out of their rooms. So it was suggested that the teenagers should be moved to large dormitory-style rooms, and that the parents with younger children should have two rooms each, which would require that the parents of the teenagers would have to give up one room apiece. Gilkey, impressed with the ingenuity of this solution, was charged with the task of presenting the proposal to the parents. None of the parents agreed to give up one of their rooms! One missionary family argued that their two teenage sons were at that stage of life where temptations abounded and hence they especially needed a good home environment. When told of the situation facing the parents of younger children, they replied, "Yes, aren't those Japanese wicked?" Another missionary argued that his sermons were important to the camp, and he needed the extra room for quietude in order to prepare his sermons. What is striking here, Gilkey notes, is not only that the people defended their self-interest, but that they found moral-sounding reasons to do so. Incidentally, this situation was also resolved by the intervention of the Japanese.

A third and final example is instructive. In January, 1945, 1550 food parcels from the American Red Cross arrived at the camp. Each parcel contained 50 pounds of food, a veritable treasure in that situation: powdered milk, butter, Spam, cheese, chocolates, sugar, coffee, jams, salmon, raisins, cigarettes. By this time, there were only 1450 people in the camp, of whom 200 were Americans. Most people therefore assumed that the 1550 parcels were intended for the whole camp. Parents excitedly told their children that soon there would be chocolates again; men dreamed of cigarettes; and mothers thought of how the jams and cheeses would brighten a very dull diet throughout the rest of the winter. The Japanese an-

LIBRARY — LUTHERAN SCHOOL
OF THEOLOGY AT CHICAGO

nounced that each person would receive one parcel, and the Americans would receive one and one-half each, since the parcels had come from the American Red Cross. On the morning of the distribution, however, the Japanese posted a sign which said, in effect, "Due to protests from the American internees, there will be no distribution." Seven Americans had gone to the authorities, protesting that all 1500 parcels should go to the 200 Americans, since the parcels were from the American Red Cross! The camp authorities wired Tokyo for instructions. Meanwhile, the effect on the camp was staggering. Bitter fathers had to explain to their children that they might not get the chocolates after all. The windfall of the parcels, which promised to provide winter-long security for everybody, had become a source of intense division because of the American concern to receive 375 pounds of food each. Gilkey, hoping that only a minority of the Americans wanted to keep all the parcels, began to visit the 200 to see if they would request the Japanese to distribute them as originally planned. The results were disappointing, though by now predictable.

One American lawyer, claiming only a professional legal interest in the case, argued that since the parcels were American property, they should be administered by Americans. An American missionary argued that there was no virtue in being forced to share; hence the Americans should be given all the parcels so that they could earn virtue by voluntarily sharing with the rest of the camp. When asked how many parcels he thought the Americans would share, he answered, "About two each," thus giving each American 5½ parcels to keep as his own as well as the virtue from sharing two! When Gilkey completed his survey, he discovered that a majority of the Americans accepted the viewpoint of the original seven protestors. Despite the fact that they had lived and suffered with the rest of the people for over two years, knowing them intimately, they refused to be swayed by persuasive moral arguments. Not only is the vividness of self-interest manifest in this episode, but the attempt to find nice-sounding reasons for that self-interest is very clear. The situation was again resolved by the intervention of Japanese power: each internee received one parcel, and the 100 extra were sent to another camp, thus costing the Americans a net loss of one-half parcel each from the original distribution plan! Gilkey comments that divine providence and judgment were operating through the Japanese authorities.

The way in which self-interest dominated reason, morality, and logic in these episodes now puts us in a position to be more direct in our estimate of human nature. Here we shall be heavily dependent on the American theologian Reinhold Niebuhr, who in turn is heavily dependent upon the Lutheran and Pauline traditions.[6]

Using the biblical story of creation, Niebuhr argues that man is created finite (out of dust) and free (in the image of God). This combination of finitude and freedom creates anxiety. Man not only has to eat; he knows that he has to eat tomorrow as well as today, and hence he becomes anxious about whether or not there will be food in the larder. This anxiety about the security of the self causes him to act to insure self-security, to put self at the center of existence rather than God (the Fall). This placing of the self at the center of existence is what is meant by "original sin." But to stop with our rather crude illustration about man's need for food is to miss the all-pervasive character of anxiety and concomitant self-interest. Man uses his reason, his power, his morality, often even his religion in the interest of the self. Man also has a boundless capacity to deceive himself, to convince himself that what he is doing is really morally and rationally correct.

What is true of the individual self is also true of social groups within a nation and the nation itself. We frequently justified our enslavement of the African by saying that we were really civilizing and Christianizing savage pagans. We used our power in our self-interest in the unscrupulous eviction and extermination of the Indian American as we expanded our frontier. Though we often describe our foreign aid program as a virtuous sharing of our wealth, the real motives are probably national security, as can be seen from the howl of protest that arises when a nation that has been receiving foreign aid from us opts for a course of action that seems antithetical to our interests. We are in favor of integrated housing until it threatens to drive our housing values down.

This understanding of self-interest as the motivating force of men may seem too harsh; so perhaps it is best to try to end with a simple example in parable form.[7] Suppose that you are arrested for traveling 35 miles per hour in a 30 miles per hour zone. No bail money is collected from you; you are simply ordered to appear in police magistrate court three days hence at 10 a.m. Suppose, furthermore, that you know that if you do not appear, the case will simply be forgotten; no warrant will be issued for your arrest, no policeman will call. Do you go down to court, or don't you? That is, out of respect for the law, and out of a knowledge that you have violated the law, do you appear? Or do you find good sounding reasons for not going? Isn't it true that most of us go to court precisely because we know that if we don't go, there will be a policeman knocking at the door? It is in our self-interest to appear, because the police have the power to do more harm to us if we don't.

In short, both our common experience and our theological tradition point to an understanding of human behavior as dominated by self-interest. This, in turn, points to the validity of the coercive or conflict approach to social change. For if men, individually and collectively, act out of self-interest, then their behavior is going to be changed primarily through the exercise of power and coercion, not through education or persuasion. Only when conflict, crisis, or coercion make it in our self-interest to change our individual behavior or societal structures is change likely to occur.

To return to the Montgomery story: though Dr. King understood himself as appealing to the conscience of the good decent majority, it was almost certainly the case that his use of power was what in fact accomplished his purpose—not his appeal to conscience.

This has profound implications for social change. It means that social change will almost always involve struggles between groups, each asserting its own self-interest; that it will involve power, conflict, and crisis.

But change and conflict do not have their origin solely in the assertion of self-interest by competing power groups. Another potent source is the rising aspirations of disinherited groups, those who hope that the future may include a more humane existence for themselves and, frequently, for all of society. This conviction that the future is open, that it may be different from the present, is summed up in the word "hope." Thus conflict is engendered not only by competition between the vested interests of the present, but between those who have a stake in preserving the present and those who hope for a better future. Theologically, one might describe this as the call of God to a new future struggling against those who wish to preserve the present or return to the past. This, however, does not change the validity of the claim that change will involve conflict, for those who wish to preserve the present and protect their own security can and normally do muster vast amounts of power to do so. The understanding of this phenomenon in the biblical tradition will be treated in our next chapter.

TOWARD A THEOLOGICAL UNDERSTANDING OF SOCIAL CHANGE

6

Throughout this book, statements of an implicitly theological or biblical character have appeared in a rather piecemeal fashion. It is now time to develop a more extensive analysis of social change from a theological and biblical point of view.

WHAT GOD IS UP TO

Such a heading must sound immodest and arrogant; yet, if we are to be loyal to God, we must attempt some answer to this question.[1] Without some answer, response to God is impossible, for what *kind* of response is one to make if one doesn't have a clue "what God is up to?"

At the heart of the biblical tradition is history—the world of cabbages and kings, of the rise and fall of empires, of sex and diapers, of change and conflict, of life and death. The biblical tradition affirms that history is the realm of religion, where God is active and where men encounter God. History, of course, is being used here not in the sense of simply the past, but in the sense of the flow of events, past, present and future, that constitute time. To say that we know God in history does not mean simply that we come to know God while we are alive, while we are in history; rather, it means that in historical events we encounter God. And that's really quite odd, but that is what the biblical tradition affirms throughout its long course, and preeminently in the Incarnation (which is the example *par excellence* that we meet God in history).

That we do not normally think of history as the realm of religion is demonstrated by a survey of a sample of the American public, over 60 percent of whom are church members. When asked, "What do you regard as the most important event in the history of the world?," the most frequent response was the discovery of America by Columbus. Tied for fourteenth with the invention of the airplane and narrowly edging out the invention of television was the birth of Christ! A proper interpretation of this survey is probably not that a majority of American Christians are hypocrites, but rather that we don't really link up history and religion. But the biblical tradition does.

Four landmark events decisively shape the history recorded in the Bible, three past and one future. They are the exodus from Egypt, the destruction of the kingdoms of Israel and Judah in the eighth and sixth centuries B.C. and the subsequent exile, and the life, death, and resurrection of Jesus of Nazareth. The fourth event, still unrealized, is the final coming of the Kingdom of God—the "eschatological" kingdom. These events are central not only because the biblical tradition would be radically different without any one of them, but also because the bulk of biblical literature is clustered around them.[2]

In canonizing the records of these four events, our fathers affirmed that they offer us the key to understanding what God is up to. In each case, God calls men out of an old style of life in community to a new style of life in community. Each involves a radical departure from the past, from the realm of sin and death to the realm

55

of life and righteousness. Hence, God is constantly active, creating new styles of human life, calling men to build new forms of human community. God is, if you will, continually bringing about social change—change, moreover, which has a direction and purpose.

Strikingly, each of these events involved more than what modern man normally labels "religion." The exodus was an event of political and economic dimensions as well as a "religious" event. Significantly, Moses did not think of religion as a private, spiritual matter, as what man does with his aloneness; if he had, he could have easily suggested that the Hebrews quietly worship God in the closets of their huts and hovels in Egypt. Undoubtedly, Pharaoh would have been much happier if Moses had believed that "religion and politics don't mix." Pharaoh's resistance came precisely from Moses' understanding that loyalty to God would bring about the economic and political liberation of those in bondage and create a new style of community life. And so we have the exodus: liberation from economic and political bondage to national life within the covenant.

Departure and new beginning are also found in the accounts of the fall of Israel and Judah and the ensuing exile. Amos is not a minority of one. His prophetic associates also speak of misplaced loyalties, social injustice, and the impending collapse of church and state. Indeed, the call of Jeremiah, which defines his whole career, points unmistakably to the theme of collapse and construction, social death and renewal:

> See, I have set you this day over nations and over kingdoms, to pluck and to break down, to destroy and to overthrow, to build and to plant (Jer. 1:10).

For the words of the prophets involved not only the collapse of an old style of community life, but the creation of a new style in exile, a life without temple, nationhood, or king.

In the New Testament, the effect of the Cross and Resurrection is the creation of a universal community, not limited by ethnic or national ties, in which there is neither Jew nor Greek, slave nor free. It is not the creation of religious individualism; it is the creation of communal

56

life so intense and so joyous that it can be referred to as one body, the body of Christ. Further, this oneness is understood as the destiny of the world.

Thus too with the final eschatological kingdom: what is hoped for is a style of life qualitatively different from the present, where every tear shall be wiped away, a style of life that is intensely communal, as exemplified in the symbol of the messianic banquet:

> And men will come from east and west, and from north and south, and sit at table in the Kingdom of God (Luke 13:29).

In the ancient Near East, eating with another was an expression of complete fellowship, far more so than our casual meals today. It is this completeness and wholeness of the human community that is hoped for in the imagery of the messianic banquet, of which the Lord's Supper is a foreshadowing. God's purpose for the world is the establishment of this messianic kingdom, whether within history or beyond. It is this destiny of the world that gives the Bible its basic dichotomy of old/new rather than good/better. Isaiah affirms, "Behold, I am doing a new thing" (Isaiah 43:19), reaffirmed by John: "Behold, I make all things new" (Rev. 21:5).

The biblical authors affirm that God is active in these events of tearing down and rebuilding: "I am the Lord your God, who brought you out of the land of Egypt" (Exodus 20:2). "I will rend and go away" (Hosea 5:14), referring to the collapse of the Northern Kingdom. "God was in Christ reconciling the world to himself" (2 Cor. 5:19). We must not imagine that God literally marched at the head of the Hebrew escapees, or literally led the foreign armies that crushed the Hebrew kingdoms. For then we could only conclude that he is inactive now, or that he did what was necessary then, but now he simply watches over his world. But the biblical writers saw in these historical events the activity of God, which they believed has a final direction: the realization of the kingdom of God. We may call this the dynamic messianism of the Bible: history moving toward a goal, guided by God.[3] And this involves social change.

CHANGE: SOME OBSERVATIONS

Having established the basic claim that social change is central to the biblical tradition, we can now make some observations about the character, purpose, and actors involved in change.

First, each of the transitions brought about by these landmark events involved conflict, in fact, the most severe form of conflict: violence. It is self-evident that the escape from Pharaoh and the subsequent conquest of Canaan involved several forms of conflict, including violence. So also with the destruction of the two kingdoms; indeed, the destruction in this case was so catastrophic as to wound the imagination: starvation, cannibalism, fire, death, and a forced march some 1000 miles into exile in Babylon. The ministry of Jesus created conflict, the cross is violence incarnate, and even that messianic kingdom, we are told, has its own birthpangs: wars and rumors of wars.

Second, times of crisis and conflict are times when God speaks to man, seeking a response. Again, this "speaking" must not be taken in a literal sense; rather, in the historical events God is calling us to a response. For example, the prophets seem to have understood the developing chaos of their day as "divine discipline," as activity of God which pointed to the destructiveness and injustice of their structures, and which called for the response of "seeking justice." This function of conflict as a call to response is clearly seen in a passage from Hosea, who spoke a few years after Amos when the crisis had become apparent to all:

> Therefore I [the Lord] am like a moth to Ephraim,
> and like dry rot to the house of Judah.
> When Ephraim saw his sickness,
> and Judah his wound,
> then Ephraim went to Assyria,
> and sent to the great king.
> But he is not able to cure you
> or heal your wound.
> For I will be like a lion to Ephraim,
> and like a young lion to the house of Judah.
> I, even I, will rend and go away,
> I will carry off, and none shall rescue.

58

I will return again to my place,
until they acknowledge their guilt
and seek my face,
and in their distress they seek me,
saying, "Come, let us return to the Lord,
for he has torn, that he may heal us;
he has stricken, and he will bind us up."

(Hos. 5:12–6:1)

The imagery in this lengthy passage is remarkable. God is like a moth, eating away the fabric of society (Ephraim is a synonym for the Northern Kingdom); God is like dry rot, weakening the structures until they collapse. In other words, the prophet interprets the domestic crisis as the activity of God. But Israel thought that she could heal herself by sending to Assyria to make a military alliance for her protection; she did not realize that her problem was domestic, and that it could not be healed by military strength. The imagery then becomes that of medicine: "The Lord has torn, that he might heal; he has stricken, and he will bind us up." In other words, the crisis is like that induced by a surgeon, intended to be healing. The crisis calls for Israel to respond to the conflict in her midst by addressing herself to the conditions that cause the anger of God; the conflict is disciplinary action, calling for correction. If Israel had realized the causes of the chaos in her midst, she would have responded appropriately, and a worse catastrophe—violent destruction—might have been avoided. She did not respond, however, and it is questionable whether Hosea thought she could.

Third, the compassion of God is directed toward the oppressed. It is in the concentration camps of Egypt that God dwelt, not in the centers of government and worship of the most powerful and generous nation of the ancient Near East. Egypt genuinely was the bread-basket of that section of the world, providing food to its neighbors in time of famine; indeed, that's how the Hebrews arrived there in the first place. But it was with the slaves that God dwelt, not with the beneficent power, and toward them that his compassion and liberating activity were directed. So too in the time of David and later King

Ahab; it was because of the fate of the lowly soldier Uriah and the small property-owner Naboth that the prophets Nathan and Elijah directed their hammerblows against the kings.

In the days of the divided kingdoms, the words of the prophets clearly indicate that the concern of God was with the slaves in the marketplace, with the victims of poverty and injustice, not in the temples of Bethel or Jerusalem, not in the summer houses or winter houses of the respectable people of God. After the collapse of those two societies, God again identified with the victims—this time with the exiles in Babylon.

In the time of Jesus, it is with the *am ha aretz*—the economically and religiously disenfranchised — that he most frequently identifies, not with the leaders of the religious and political establishment of the day. Some of the most memorable statements in the Gospels manifest this concern of God with the oppressed. For example, the words of Mary in the Magnificat sum it up well:

> *He has brought down monarchs from their thrones,*
> *but the humble have been lifted high.*
> *The hungry he has satisfied with good things,*
> *the rich sent empty away (Luke 1:52-53, NEB).*

Or in the words of the Beatitudes:

> *How blest are you who are in need; the kingdom of*
> *   God is yours.*
> *How blest are you who now go hungry; your hunger*
> *   shall be satisfied.*
> *How blest are you who weep now; you shall laugh*
> *   (Luke 6:20-21, NEB).*

The world which the biblical writers knew presupposed a vertical social order of classes—poor, middle class, wealthy—and the God of the biblical tradition is regularly with those at the bottom of that ladder. That may sound harsh, but it is difficult to escape that conclusion

Why is there this identification? Not because such groups are any better morally (as the exodus tradition makes clear, the slaves were a "stiff-necked" people), nor because they have special rights, but probably because they do not have the power necessary to defend themselves against the abuses of others. And, to be sure, God *does* care about the "fat cats" as well; he cares that we might discover the conflicts in our midst as a call to us, that we might recover our humanity, a humanity which cannot be found in a fragmented world whose broken existence is often legitimized by our rationalizations. That is, to say that God loved the *world* means that I cannot find wholeness apart from my brother. This compassion of God for the oppressed offers us a clear clue as to what he is calling us to in the conflicts of our time.

Fourth, the biblical figures are active in producing conflict and social change. This is self-evidently the case with Moses, who began by using channels (the many requests to Pharaoh), before the exercise of power became necessary. But it is also true of the prophets. Frequently they are seen primarily as announcers of crisis; but an inspection of the Old Testament understanding of "word" shows that they are active as well.

In the world of the Old Testament, a very exalted conception of the power of a "word" operated; this was particularly true when the "word" in question was spoken on solemn occasions, as an oath or blessing, or when it was claimed that it was a "word" from God. On such occasions, it was believed that the "word" spoken was irrevocable, and that it even helped to bring into being that about which it spoke. We can illustrate this with the familiar story of Jacob stealing his father's blessing from his brother Esau. Esau, as the oldest son, was entitled to it. But as the blind aged father Isaac lies on his bed, Jacob deceives Isaac by masquerading as Esau, and Isaac pronounces the word of blessing upon Jacob. When Esau returns, Isaac discovers what has happened and, we are told, he trembled violently. Esau cries out in anguish, "with an exceedingly great and bitter cry, and said to his father 'Bless me, even me also, O my father!'" (Genesis 27:34). But as the rest of the story makes clear, Isaac cannot. Why? One would think he could say, "Well, it was a mistake to give it to Jacob, and besides that, he deceived me as well, so I'll give it to Esau." But he can't —because a word once spoken cannot be revoked, and because it creates that of which it speaks.

When it was the "word of God" that was being uttered

the irrevocability and efficaciousness were even more intense. Hence, when a prophet spoke of the coming collapse of his society, both he and the people believed that he was assisting in bringing the event nearer; in short, he was a revolutionary actor. One might regard this understanding of "word" as a primitive suspicion stemming from ancient culture, as magic unworthy of our attention, but the fact that the people believed it is what matters, for it means that both prophet and people thought of the prophet as an actor, not just a speaker.

The role of the prophets as actors is even more evident when they perform what Old Testament scholars term a "prophetic act." Here the prophet acts out what is to happen. This was believed to add to the already emphatic efficaciousness of the spoken word; it was not simply dramatic embellishment. For example, in Jeremiah 19-20, Jeremiah takes a vase which symbolizes Jerusalem, smashes it to the ground and announces, "Thus says the Lord of hosts: so will I break this people and this city" (Jeremiah 19:11). The biblical tradition is full of figures active in radical social change. Since they understood themselves to be doing the will of God, God is actually the revolutionary actor, the bringer of social change, with the bibical figures his servants in change. That is even more striking.

We can now summarize these observations. "What God is up to" is that he is continually creating new styles of life in community, which inevitably involves change and conflict. These times of conflict are times when God is calling men to respond to his activity, calling men to be active in the change which he is bringing about. His compassion is directed especially to the oppressed, and his purpose is the binding up of the fragmented human community, reconciling man to man and to himself in the universal community of being.

THE NATURE OF SOCIAL STRUCTURES

By social structures we mean the state, laws, customs, classes, etc. The biblical attitude toward such structures might appear to be negative; i.e., they are simply to be destroyed. But the attitude is not quite that simple.

We must begin by drawing attention to some rather odd terms in St. Paul's writings. Paul often speaks of principalities, powers, elemental spirits of the universe, authority, rule, and the prince of the power of the air. Literature outside of the New Testament shows that these were quite common expressions in the Mediterranean world, and that they seemed to refer to angelic or demonic beings. But a closer study of St. Paul shows that he uses these terms to account for rather ordinary phenomena: the state, law, customs, death, guilt, perhaps disease. And hence this language is really about what we would call social structures (the state, laws, customs), though it includes more.

What then is Paul's attitude toward these principalities and powers? They seem to have a useful purpose; i.e., they were created by God. But Paul is equally convinced that they have strayed from their original usefulness; created to serve man, they have in fact become man's masters, holding him in bondage (in modern terms, social structures are meant to be made for man, not man for the structures). Man has become dehumanized, held in bondage by the principalities and powers.

But bondage is not the last word. For Paul understands that in the death and resurrection of Christ, something has begun which will be completed at "the end." Two verses make this clear:

> He disarmed the principalities and powers and made a public example of them, triumphing over them in him (Col. 2:15).

> Then comes the end, when he delivers the kingdom to God the Father after destroying every rule and every authority and power (I Cor. 15:24).

In the first passage, the specific principalities and powers which were exposed seem to be the religious and political establishments of the first century, which were in fact the best religious and political institutions of the ancient world. Of course, there is an echo in this verse of the other principalities and powers as well. But the point is that the best social structures were exposed as less than ultimate, as imperfect. The second passage speaks of the eventual fate of such structures. In the interim, which is the time in which we live, the followers of Christ are to seek to ensure that structures serve men rather than men serving structures. And hence the question for our time becomes: what structures of society dehumanize men, holding them in bondage? How can they become humanized? It is striking to note how what are often separated into the "spiritual" and "social" sides of the gospel are here firmly united in Paul's understanding of the powers. For that which dehumanizes man, that from which God is concerned to release man, includes sin and guilt as well as social structures, like tyranny, poverty, prejudice, or class structures.

RADICAL MONOTHEISM

The fourth and final key to understanding social change perhaps belongs theologically first. But we have put it last to appreciate its significance.

Radical monotheism is admirably summed up in the confession of Israel: "Hear, O Israel: The Lord our God is one Lord; and you shall love the Lord your God with all your heart, and with all your soul, and with all your might" (Deut. 6:4-5). It is also stated in the First Commandment, and in the early Christian confession, "Jesus is Lord." We are to have one power to whom we are loyal and in whom we trust.

There are two consequences of radical monotheism for social change. The first is that it relativizes every human institution or structure. If one has only one center of ultimate or highest loyalty, then one cannot give ultimate or final loyalty to any finite institution, whether it be the state, the church, the family, a given social structure, or a given economic system. One can at best have a secondary loyalty to such institutions, a loyalty which may be called into question and nullified by one's ultimate loyalty to God.

One way to illustrate this is by examining Luther's explanation of the First Commandment in his Large Catechism. Luther comments, "That to which your heart clings and entrusts itself is, I say, really your God." "To have a god is nothing else than to trust and believe him

64

with our whole heart." [4] In other words, whatever we cling to and trust in for security is our god; if what we cling to and trust in is our country, or the American way of life, or the church, or our own intelligence, or our family, then that has really become our god, which, of course, is what the radical monotheism of the Hebrew-Christian tradition prohibits. Luther goes on: "The heart should know no other consolation or confidence than that in him, nor let itself be torn from him, but for him should risk and disregard everything else on earth." [5]

Here Luther envisions the possibility that loyalty to God and loyalty to finite institutions may conflict; when that happens, one is to be loyal to God, even if that means being disloyal to those institutions which we may hold dear. This implication of radical monotheism is sometimes called the "desacralizing of institutions," and it may in fact be part of the cause of modern social change. For if no institution is sacred, then it is up to man to design and arrange institutions so that they serve man. Every institution and structure is open to judgment and change, because God alone is perfect and God alone deserves our final loyalty.

Besides opening every finite structure to change, the second implication of radical monotheism has to do with the well-being of the actor involved in change. When the whole world is collapsing, when everything in which one had found one's security is changing and perhaps even disappearing, when everything seems new and unfamiliar, where does one find one's identity, one's security, one's freedom? Only by having one's security in that which transcends everything finite, namely God. For if one has one's security primarily in the fact that one is an American, or a German, or a black man or white man, then one is really subject to the preservation of "American-ness," "German-ness," blackness, whiteness; one is in bondage to those phenomena. One can be free only by having one's security in that which is indestructible, which neither moth nor mildew nor rust can touch — God. Thus radical monotheism liberates one from final dependence on any finite phenomenon. In short, it is the source for the freedom of the actor.

WHERE IS PEACE OF MIND?

This chapter suggests that a primary task of the Christian is to be involved in social and political tasks, in social conflicts, in humanizing the world, in wrestling with the principalities and powers, engaged in the conflict that flows out of loyalty to the messianic vision. That's striking, and may run counter to some of our central religious understandings. Most prominently, where is the peace of mind in that?

> *Where are the consolations of religion? Where is the comfort it promises; the peace that passes understanding — what has happened to it? Does religion exist only to dislocate man from his environment, to pit him against his brother, to make him so uneasy with human life that he indulges in unsettling protest?* [6]

These are valid questions. That is, though they may reflect a religious environment that has been over-filled with the rhetoric of peace of mind, there are also those genuine elements in our tradition that speak of peace: "The peace of God, which passes all understanding, will keep your hearts and your minds in Christ Jesus" (Philippians 4:7); "The Lord bless you and keep you: The Lord make his face shine upon you, and be gracious to you: The Lord lift up his countenance upon you, and give you peace." What happens to these elements if the theology we have outlined illuminates in any way the task of the Christian?

Two points need to be made in reply to this legitimate question. First, as suggested earlier, the call to social action is not the whole of theology. It emphasizes the prophetic element in theology rather than the pastoral. But the pastoral element urgently needs the prophetic element, else we shall find the Christian task to be concerned primarily with ministering to the real and imagined psychiatric disorders of man.

Second, most of the biblical actors didn't have what we popularly imagine to be peace of mind. Jeremiah surely didn't; he could exclaim, "My anguish, my anguish, I writhe in pain"; he could accuse God of being as useless as a dry stream bed, which is pretty useless in a land as arid as Judah. Then there is Jesus; he surely cannot be pictured as a serene figure gliding undisturbed and unmoved by the agonies of existence. What kind of peace of mind is there in the cry, "My God, my God, why hast thou forsaken me?" Or St. Paul, whose experience of anguish, beatings, imprisonments, and conflicts with other religious figures must be some sort of record. If peace of mind and security still seem like what religion should offer, then perhaps we need to remember that some of the best Christian literature was written behind bars.

What this suggests is that the peace promised by the Hebrew-Christian tradition is either an eschatological hope, to be realized only in the messianic kingdom, or it is a peace that transcends the agonies of finitude without negating them. In any case, the quest for the consolation of religion ought not be sought apart from the prophetic task, but must be found within that task.

Besides suggesting that the Christian as individual is called to take part in the transformation of the world, this chapter may also imply that the church is to be understood as an agent of social and political action. Not only does that sound unfamiliar, but it's rather jarring and audacious. We must leave a consideration of the church's task until the concluding chapter.

THE NATURE AND FUNCTIONS OF CONFLICT

7

Not only is conflict an inevitable aspect of social change, but it has several useful functions as well about which we must speak. But first some more precise definitions are necessary.

SOME DEFINITIONS

The closely related terms violence, power, and conflict are used in a bewildering number of ways, both in our common speech and in the more technical works of social scientists. Because there are a variety of definitions possible, we shall specify in what senses we are using the terms. Since we will be using the terms violence and power in our clarification of conflict, we shall begin by defining those two terms.

Violence is used in this book in the commonly accepted sense of an open clash involving the use of power in ways that involve physical harm to life or property. It can, of course, be either legal or illegal.

Power is the attempt to affect another person's or group's behavior against his or its will. It can be either regulated (as in the case of police enforcing a law) or unregulated (as in the case of a boycott, strike, etc.). It should be noted that power and violence are not synonyms; violence is one form of power, but there are also non-violent forms of power. In this book, coercion is a synonym for power.

Conflict is defined in both a narrow and broad sense in contemporary social science.[1] The narrow definition refers only to open clashes or struggles, either violent or non-violent. The broad definition includes such manifest struggles, but also tensions, hostile attitudes, and antagonistic interests between groups, even if those phenomena have not resulted in open struggle.

The danger of a narrow definition is that it tends to focus all of one's attention on dealing with the immediate struggle or crisis (to which the unfortunate answer may be a repressive form of law and order), rather than focusing our attention on the underlying issues that create such open conflict. That is, the narrow definition may in fact limit what we see in a given situation. Hence we shall define conflict in the broad sense.

We will, however, make a distinction within the category of conflict. *Overt or open conflict* refers to the open use of, or threat to use, power, whereas *latent conflict* refers to the previously-mentioned tensions, hostile attitudes, and antagonistic interests.

The usefulness of such a broad definition of conflict can be clarified by an example. Often the person or group who introduces overt conflict into a situation is labeled the villain, the troublemaker, or agitator. But such an allegation can be sustained only if one is operating with a very narrow definition of conflict. Our broader definition enables us to see that most frequently the instigator of overt conflict is only making manifest the latent conflict of a stultifying status quo. Thus, properly speaking, he does not introduce conflict into a previously peaceful situation; the conflict, in its latent form, was already there. Or, to put it differently, he does not create

69

the fire of conflict; he points to the already seething cauldron.

If we can bear one more distinction, conflict can also be spoken of as realistic or non-realistic. *Realistic conflict* is directed at the attainment of a specific end. *Non-realistic conflict* is conflict engaged in as an end in itself. This distinction will become important later on.[2]

THE FUNCTIONS OF OVERT CONFLICT

The last chapters stressed the inevitability of conflict to such an extent that conflict might sound like a necessary and tragic evil, a demonic aspect of human existence. To be sure, conflict clearly has its unlovely side, but it also has creative uses:

> We may say that conflict undealt with is bad (not that conflict is bad, but that the consequences of not dealing with it are bad), but conflict recognized, accepted and dealt with is a sign of maturity.[3]

In short, the inevitability of conflict is not to be lamented, but should be seen as laden with creative potential. We must now discuss these functions, weaving together insights from sociology, the Montgomery boycott, and the biblical tradition.

THE CREATIVE POTENTIAL OF CONFLICT

Conflict is a means of articulate political protest. Self-evidently, this was the case in Montgomery. It drew attention in an unmistakable manner to those practices which the black community viewed as unjust. It is particularly useful in those situations where normal channels are either closed, or where the structures are so rigid that normal means of change prove ineffective.

Whether we would call Amos and his fellow prophets political protestors is debatable, since that is a rather modern term. But clearly they do speak for the oppressed of their society at the very same time that they speak for God.

Conflict is a "safety valve." The term "safety valve" is

used with some caution here. It is meant in the sense that conflict calls attention to the presence of unaddressed grievances; it is an indication that tension exists in the community. It should not be understood in the sense of a simple release from tension, for then the condition producing the overt conflict would still remain. If the unaddressed grievances are attended to, then conflict will have served the purpose of preventing a more intense and perhaps catastrophic conflict. In short, it may prevent conflict from escalating from realistic forms, where a specific goal is sought, to non-realistic forms, where people are attacked rather than specific goals being sought. An excellent and chilling example of the escalation from realistic to non-realistic forms of conflict can be seen in Frantz Fanon's book *The Wretched of the Earth*. Fanon argues that the experience of the African native at the hands of European colonialists has been so humiliating, brutal, and long-lived that only massive violence against the representatives of the colonial powers can serve as a means of recapturing the humanity of the oppressed. This is tragic, but it is a situation that has perhaps grown inevitably out of long-suppressed grievances. If conflict can prevent such a situation from developing, it will genuinely have served the whole community.

This is clearly one of the functions of conflict in the biblical tradition, especially as seen in the lengthy passage from Hosea in the previous chapter. There Israel was called to respond to the latent conflict in her midst; she did not, and inevitably it escalated into overt and violent conflict. Thus the faithful community is meant to understand that conflicts are intended to call attention to conditions which grieve God. Conflict, in short, calls us to respond.

Conflict creates a new sense of identity for the actors. This is often true for both groups and individuals, particularly when the victims of injustice may have begun to doubt their own humanity because of their oppression. It can be illustrated by what happened to the black people of Montgomery. Before the boycott, Dr. King describes the feelings of the black community:

> *. . perhaps an even more basic force at work was their corroding sense of inferiority, which often expressed itself in a lack of self-respect.*[4]

During and after the boycott, a quite different sense of identity developed. After indictments had been issued for the arrest of over 100 black people who were participating in the boycott,

> *No one, it seems, had been frightened. No one had tried to evade arrest. Many Negroes had gone voluntarily to the sheriff's office to see if their names were on the list, and were even disappointed when they were not. A once fear-ridden people had been transformed. Those who had previously trembled before the law were now proud to be arrested for the cause of freedom. . . . They [the city] thought they were dealing with a group who could be cajoled or forced to do whatever the white man wanted them to do. They were not aware that they were dealing with Negroes who had been freed from fear. . . . Their methods were geared to the "old Negro," and they were dealing with a "new Negro."*[5]

Thus conflict often creates a new awareness of "Who am I?" which in the case of victimized groups is crucial. This new sense of identity even became manifest in outward appearance:

> *. . . there is still a feeling of closeness among the various classes and ages and religious denominations that was never present before. The increased self-respect of even the least sophisticated Negroes in Montgomery is evident in the way they dress and walk, in new standards of cleanliness and of general deportment.*[6]

Similar evidence can be added from many individuals who have engaged in social conflict. In the case of the movement against the Vietnam war, many who have participated have discovered a new sense of who they are. After being involved in the struggle against the war for some time and finally turning in his draft card, one college student wrote:

72

I feel a freedom that I've never known — and a faith that I've never felt before, a faith that tells me I can do what I think is right without being anxious about the personal consequences that will follow.

What this suggests is that in conflict, one discovers what one is willing to stand for, how much one is willing to risk, how free and authentic one really is; in short, one discovers who one is. Note that engaging in social conflict, particularly when standing against a superior power, appears filled with risk and danger, yet the result is often fulfillment, wholeness, freedom. This is not to glorify conflict; on the other hand, such testimony may be an experimental verification of the familiar, "Whoever loses his life . . . will find it."

Conflict brings together previously unrelated groups. First, it brings together the opposing parties, who previously may have had no relationship, or else only a perverted relationship of dominance-submission. They may face each other across the negotiating table as hostile groups, but they do at least establish communication. This often leads to a degree of mutual respect and eventual amicable cooperation. This is clearly the case in labor-management relationships in the United States. The hostility and violence which once characterized the relationships of those two groups has been replaced by a generally cooperative spirit — indeed, so cooperative that many radicals accuse labor of having sold out. In Montgomery, though there were relationships between blacks and whites, they were largely unofficial and fell into the dominant-submissive pattern. During the boycott, however, the MIA negotiated with the city as equals, and the firm resolve of the black people actually changed the character of the relationship:

> *Today [1958] the Negro citizen in Montgomery is respected in a way that he never was before. In the calm aftermath of the crisis many local white people are ready to say what they felt they could not say while the struggle was going on: "We've got to hand it to those Negroes. They had principles and they stuck to them and they stuck together. They organized and planned well."* [7]

73

Thus, not only does conflict establish new relationships, but it frequently leads to mutual respect, cooperation, and, eventually, perhaps, affection. Conflict is thus one step in the process of reconciliation.

If conflict brings opponents together, it also creates alliances between like-minded people who formerly may have been separated by various barriers. The movement which began in Montgomery and spread throughout the nation frequently brought together black, white, clergy, labor, housewives, students — an assortment of people not previously related. To be sure, this has disintegrated (at least superficially) in the rise of a more militant black movement. Yet the alliance still exists. In Montgomery itself, the badly-fragmented black community was brought together:

> Physicians, teachers, and lawyers sat or stood beside domestic workers and unskilled laborers. The Ph.D.'s and the no "D's" were bound together in a common venture. The so-called "big Negroes" who owned cars and had never ridden the buses came to know the maids and the laborers who rode the buses every day. Men and women who had been separated from each other by false standards of class were now singing and praying together in a common struggle.[8]

Conflict creates the possibility of a new society. That is, conflict creates the possibility of new structures, new laws, new power relationships.

First, conflict often revitalizes norms that have been dormant, forgotten, or ignored. It leads us to rediscover elements of our heritage. For many Americans, the black struggle has led them to discover the expression of theoretical equality found in the American creed. It has led the Supreme Court to revitalize standards that, it argues, are implicitly contained in the Constitution and its amendments. So too in the history of the church: conflict has invariably led to a recapturing of insights that had been forgotten, as in the Reformation re-emphasis on grace, scripture, and faith, or in the re-emphasis on our oneness in Christ that is the wellspring of the modern ecumenical movement. The application of these rediscovered norms, whether in church or the world (to use an increasingly artificial distinction), modifies and re-juvenates the institutions involved.

So too in the biblical tradition. In the midst of conflict, Amos calls his community back to their wellsprings: remember that you were slaves in Egypt, and God freed you! After the fall of Jerusalem in 586 B.C., the community in exile was also forced to reflect on its beginnings and purpose. If, as they affirmed, the conflict that they had just experienced was the will of God, what should they do? They must, they affirmed, rededicate themselves to obedience to God. Furthermore, since conflict had deprived them of both temple and king (church and state), they came to discover what was really essential:

> He has showed you, O man, what is good;
> and what does the Lord require of you
> but to do justice, and to love kindness,
> and to walk humbly with your God (Micah 6:8)?

It also led them to rediscover that the faithful community had a universal purpose in history, as is marvelously demonstrated in the pages of Isaiah 40-66, written during and after the exile. There, expressed with new vividness, is the claim that the faithful community is to be a light to the nations through the path of suffering and servant-hood. This perception arose out of the throes of conflict.

Second, conflict often creates a new framework of norms. In the political realm, this is most evident in the case of new legislation. Legislation almost always comes as a response to conflict. Hence the character of the society is redefined through new protections and new aids provided by law.

Third, conflict can establish a more viable balance of power, which makes a more just society possible. His-torians have long noted that justice in society is best achieved through the presence of a rough balance of power. In the absence of such a balance of power, the strong are tempted to exploit the weak, and the weak have no way of preventing such exploitation. King notes that this was one of the results of the boycott. The city of Montgomery feared initiating any further prosecution for violations of segregation laws, because they suspected that the black community would protest and appeal any convictions to the Supreme Court. Thus the new-found power of the black community caused at least some of the previous injustice to be ameliorated. Even the most blatant manifestation of white supremacy, the Ku Klux Klan, found that its status had been redefined. Formerly, black people had been terrified of the Klan, and their mere appearance would cause blacks to flee the streets. But their appearance after the success of the boycott was greeted by a black community that simply went about its business, neither reacting in fear nor retaliation.

The above five claims about conflict should amply demonstrate that it can be a creative tool of the attempt to establish a human community. Clearly it can be brutal, of course. Indeed, one possible result of conflict is annihilation, and it is this possibility that makes conflict seem so threatening. But if our chapter has demonstrated anything, it should have made clear that what threatens society is not conflict itself, but rigid and oppressive structures which permit hostilities to accumulate.

In theological terms, what threatens the human community is not conflict, but the refusal of people to be willing to move into the future which God is creating, the contentment with the present realm of injustice and death rather than responding to God's call to life and righteousness.

ON VIOLENCE

Rapid social change and conflict do not necessarily involve violence, as we have seen, though they often do or at least threaten to do so. Such violence, when practiced by the agents of change, is almost always illegal. What is the appropriate Christian response in such a situation? This is an exceedingly troublesome dilemma, and it is very difficult to suggest the appropriate response. But there are some distinctions and observations to be made that can at least clarify the dilemma.

We must distinguish between spontaneous violence and programmed or planned violence. Spontaneous violence, by definition, erupts without conscious planning or foresight. It is frequently an expression of utter frustration. Since it is not a planned part of a movement, it would seem that Christians would be ill-advised to abandon a movement or its aims simply because acts of spontaneous violence have occurred. When such abandonment does occur, one suspects that the person simply wanted a way out and the eruption of violence provided a ready and moral-sounding excuse.

But in the case of the threat or use of programmed violence, the situation is less clear. Here sniping, sabotage, arson, perhaps guerilla warfare, may be regular occurrences. Few if any readers of this book will face this dilemma as a participant; but what about our attitudes from a distance toward such movements? Is it ever appropriate for a Christian to aid such movements, whether it's a black revolutionary movement in South Africa or a revolution in Latin America, or some future movement in the United States? Many of our fellow Christians are caught in that dilemma right now; for example, in Latin America a considerable number of priests and laity must decide for or against such movements. We too are implicated, for the magnitude of our country's economic and military interests means that in almost every case we are supporting those who are suppressing such movements. Hence it's not simply an academic question: we are involved by the very complexity of the human web in which we live. What can be said?

First, violence is usually due to the failure to address the issues raised by non-violent forms of conflict. In most cases, it is the blindness or the contentment or the stubbornness of those in power which allows a situation to escalate from one that can be resolved by non-violent conflict to one in which violence erupts. Hence the presence of violence is a judgment upon a system's failure as well as a potent reason for addressing grievances before they result in violence.

Second, one must recognize the destructiveness that is caused in some systems. For example, we now know that lack of protein during early childhood can permanently impede the development of a child's intelligence, not only preventing him from assuming a productive role in a society that increasingly calls for sophisticated skills, but also violating him as a human being. Literally millions of parents today face the agony of watching their children suffer such deficiency because of the inequities of the present structures. Thus it is not realistic to assume that the revolutionary is introducing destruction into a basically non-destructive environment. Instead, one has to ask, might the amount of destructiveness produced by a violent revolution be less than the amount of destructiveness produced by the continuation of a stratified and stagnant status quo? That is a question which can only be answered in relationship to specific situations.

Third, unless the Christian is a pacifist, the Christian does admit that there are some conditions under which it is responsible to take a life; e.g., to protect the neighbor from unjust aggression. Historically, most Christians have granted the propriety of such overt violence in specific situations. This means that one cannot oppose revolutionary violence simply on the grounds that it is violent *unless,* as stated earlier, one is a pacifist, opposed to all violence in principle and in practice. Ironically, many of those who condemn revolution on the grounds that it's violent are only too ready to kill in the name of the state.

Fourth, we must recognize that most of us are reaping the fruits of a society that was established through revolutionary violence (American, French, Russian, English, Chinese). This alone does not mean that revolutionary violence is legitimate, of course. But it does mean that if we condemn revolution in principle as wrong, we are then pronouncing the act which generated our society as illegitimate, as one that ought not have happened.

Fifth, under some historical conditions, violence can be functional; that is, it can produce beneficial results rather than simply repression. A contemporary historian concludes:

> The historian is obliged to conclude that collective violence, including the recent riots in black ghettos, has often quickened the disposition of those in power to redress just grievances.[9]

Hence the common objection that violence only causes an even greater and more repressive counter-violence is not always true.

But though these observations may clarify the issues and nullify the effect of some commonly heard objections, the dilemma still remains: can Christian love of the neighbor ever legitimately express itself in programmed revolutionary violence? Convinced of the immense violation done to human life by some existing structures, a recent church conference concluded:

> Therefore the question often emerges today whether the violence which sheds blood in planned revolutions may not be a lesser evil than the violence which, though bloodless, condemns whole populations to perennial despair.[10]

A second conference went slightly beyond the posing of the dilemma to conclude, with great hesitation and caution:

> Dare we leave the roads to justice and peace so blocked that men who look to the future have to resort to violence where other ways are possible? It is the work of courageous dynamic love to break through these rigidities. There can be non-violent revolutions. All our efforts must be directed to change without violence. But if injustice is so embedded in the status quo and its supporters refuse to permit change, then as a last resort men's conscience may lead them in full and clear sighted responsibility without hate or rancour to engage in violent revolution. A heavy burden then rests on those who have resisted change.[11]

Here is an explicit recognition that violent revolution may be justified. Yet it is utterly essential to leave the single sentence that approves revolution within its carefully-worded context; otherwise the statement will have a more bloodthirsty connotation than it in fact carries. Note especially how the obligation to use non-violent methods is stressed, methods which include the whole spectrum from persuasion to voting to boycotts to protests to social disruption. Only when these have been exhausted, the paragraph concludes, may men in good conscience resort to programmed violence.

Clearly, there is still discomfort about that prospect.

Violence is messy business; lives are at stake; the consequences of violence are often unpredictable. If one were deeply evangelical, perhaps he would say, "The grace of God permits me to dirty my hands for the sake of my neighbor, and that includes the dirty business of revolutionary violence." That is, I am not saved by keeping my shirt-tails clean from the blood of revolutionary violence; I am saved by the grace of God. Yet, to reconcile such violence with the biblical concern about the total well-being of men is difficult. But if one affirms that the gospel leads one to reject revolutionary violence, the answer cannot be a withdrawal from the throes of change and conflict. If love of my neighbor and loyalty to God impel me to eschew violence, then love of my neighbor and loyalty to God impel me to lay my life on the line for the well-being of others in creative and adventurous acts of non-violence. In other words, the alternative to violence is not non-involvement; the alternative is militant use of non-violent means.

THE CHRISTIAN THE CHURCH AND SOCIAL CHANGE

8

It is now necessary to speak about the involvement of Christians in social change and conflict. The purpose of the preceding portion of this book has been to demonstrate that there is biblical warrant for and call to such involvement. In this chapter, we shall speak first about Christians *as individuals* who become involved in conflict and change, and second about the role of the church *as an institution,* whether on the inter-denominational, denominational, or local parish level.

THE INDIVIDUAL CHRISTIAN

Individual Christians frequently find themselves involved in situations where conflict (not necessarily violence, to recall our earlier distinctions) has already broken out. Indeed, all of us at this particular time in history are in such a situation; there are only differences in degree of involvement, and in attitude toward involvement. In addition, individual Christians may find themselves part of a movement which initiates overt conflict, or may decide to become part of such a movement. But whether the involvement is unavoidable or voluntarily chosen, there are certain resources in the Christian tradition which have direct relevance to the creative handling of conflict.

THE UNDERSTANDING OF SIN WITH WHICH WE HAVE TO DEAL

The biblical tradition of the Fall provides us with our first resource. It points to the self-interest in all of our actions, as well as to the self-interest present in our institutions. It points to our limited perspectives, colored by self-interest and contentment, which lead us to overlook unaddressed grievances. It also suggests that easy solutions will not be found, since the actions of both oppressed and oppressor are affected by self-interest. In light of the reality of sin, at least four implications follow for the creative handling of conflict.

First, the response to an eruption of conflict should be one of repentance, even if, at first glance, it appears that the "fault" is on the other side. For, except in the most extraordinary situations, "fault" is not reserved to one side. Social conflict does not erupt unless there are some grievances; hence its presence points to our guilt, as individuals and as a church and society.

But in saying that repentance is called for, we have to guard against remorse or grief becoming a substitute for concrete action. This identification of repentance with remorse is thoroughly unbiblical, for repentance implies not only remorse but also a turning away from the past and turning toward the future. But it frequently happens that our response to conflict is exhausted in an orgy of breast-beating which leaves the situation much as it was before. It is possible to interpret the national outpouring of grief following the assassinations of Robert Kennedy and Martin Luther King in precisely these terms. For three days, the nation agonized over the possible meanings of those events, but then, its catharsis complete, went back to normal. But repentance in the full sense of recognizing that something is wrong and recognizing our own responsibility for it, coupled with a resolve to address the problem, is still the first necessary response.

Second, our recognition of the depth of sin will lead us to attack "systems" rather than individuals. For we are, to a large extent, conditioned to act as we do by the institutions of which we are a part. Hence, to engage in actions against individuals, whether by name-calling or more drastic means, really misses the point. Perhaps this can be illustrated from the scene of industrial relations.

> In an industrial dispute, personalities become involved and people are attacked as people rather than as functionaries of a particular viewpoint, precisely because they have not accepted that conflict is natural, that it is a built-in part of the system.[1]

In other words, personal hostilities and animosities can be decreased by the recognition that the other person is not an "evil" man; to a large extent, he acts as he does because of the system of which he is a part, a system that inevitably includes the institutionalization of self-interest.

Third, a recognition of the sin with which we have to deal implies that power will have to be used in bringing about change, for reasons described in an earlier chapter. The ways of using power for an individual Christian are many: voting, writing letters to representatives of government, participation in government, support with contributions, participation in protests or boycotts, civil disobedience, using one's present institutional position to bring about change, etc. The recognition of the necessity of using power prevents us from a noble yet sentimental "wishing" that things might be better.

Fourth, the recognition of sin entails that we ruthlessly examine our own positions to see where rationalizations due to self-interest are operating. This is true whether we identify ourselves with the preservers of the status quo or with those seeking change. To what extent are my own most cherished notions really a product of my self-interest? But such examination must not lead to paralysis, for fear that we might really be acting selfishly. If that happened, then we would have a magnificent example of using the doctrine of original sin in a self-interested way — namely, to prevent action! What is called for is ruthless honesty, followed by activity.

THE CHRISTIAN IDEAL OF OTHER-DIRECTEDNESS

Earlier we spoke of the radical freedom from self and for the other person that stems from loyalty to God. What this means is that defense of the ego not only cannot be, but need not be, primary.

Perhaps this can be illustrated by reference to the racial crisis in our own nation. In the early sixties, many whites were quite pleased and excited about being involved with the movement. But this has changed to a large extent with the emergence of the rhetoric of black power and black militancy, when all whites are frequently lumped together as racists. How ought one respond to this?

One can respond by saying, "I don't like it," or "Don't they realize that we're not all like that?" The usual consequence of such a statement is withdrawal from involvement. But what is really happening here is that withdrawal, understandable as it is, is occurring because of a bruised ego; "they" aren't treating me fairly any more; "they" aren't grateful for what I've done. But to withdraw for this reason is an irrelevant response. The important question is not, "Do I like it?", but rather, "What's happening, and how should I respond to what's happening?" Furthermore, it is loyalty to God and the consequent freedom from putting the ego first that makes such a response possible.

THE CHRISTIAN IDEAL OF RECONCILIATION

The biblical view is that conflict is not the goal; beyond conflict lies reconciliation. This affirmation has several implications for the individual Christian in conflict.

First, it means that there is a ministry to be performed to the person who is fearful of change or conflict (and that probably means most of us). He needs to be shown that the attack is not against him as a person, but upon an injustice to which he may be unwittingly contributing.

84

Even if he should, in full knowledge and intention, be perpetuating the injustice, he is not to be viewed as beyond the sphere of reconciliation; he is still a person to be reconciled.

This distinction between persons and systems is admittedly a difficult one to put into practice. The severe language of the prophets is often directed against individuals, as are also the "woes" to the religious establishment in the Gospels (Matt. 23, Luke 11). Yet, difficult as it may be to practice it in all situations, it is possible to practice it in many situations, and it must be a goal in all situations. Perhaps a minimum that is possible in all situations is to assure the person that the attack is not against him personally, but against what he represents.

Second, the goal of reconciliation implies that we must listen seriously to the other person and seek to understand his position. If the person believes strongly in something, there must be a reason for it, and we owe it to him as a person to discover why. If the other person won't even talk, there must be reasons for that too, and an exploration of those reasons may reopen channels of communication.

HOPE

Hope is a dominant element of the biblical tradition. Its application to individuals in change and conflict can be very succinctly stated. It is the conviction that God is at work, even when the evidence seems to suggest otherwise. No situation is literally "hope-less," for, the Christian affirms, "Jesus is Lord," and ultimately nothing can frustrate his lordship.

Essential as this hope is, it can be illegitimately used. For hope can be conceived of as resignation to what God wills, which amounts to acquiescence to the present state of affairs. Instead, hope should lead to the conviction that there is no situation which is unchanging; that it always makes sense to work for improvement, even when it seems, humanly speaking, impossible. Hope can lead us to look for unexpected cracks in the present structures, to use our imaginations, and to trust that our efforts ultimately make sense. Without such a hope, the tragic dead-end of despair and cynicism is too easily reached.

85

THE CHURCH: OBJECT AND INSTRUMENT OF SOCIAL CHANGE

The church as an institution (local parish, synod, denomination, national or international council) is at least two-sided. On the one hand, it is to be the pilgrim people of God, witnessing to and being an instrument of his activity in the world. On the other hand, it also stands in constant need of reformation, since it is always imperfect. That is, it contains the inhibitions of the people who constitute it. Thus the church not only is an instrument of social change; it also stands in need of change itself. We are thus faced with two questions: how can the church change itself, and how can it be the leaven in the world, changing the world?

Before addressing these questions, it is necessary to recognize the magnitude of the problem, at least in skeletal terms. This means that we must be very honest in describing the situation of the church today. Much of what we must say is harsh, but it is a solid, if uncomfortable, biblical principle that God's judgment begins with the House of Israel — i.e., with those who adhere to the Hebrew-Christian tradition.

First, especially where a majority of the people are affiliated with the church, the church normally reflects the culture in which it lives rather than changing or standing against that culture. This is not surprising, since the church is composed of people who breathe deeply of that culture. Hence the biases, prejudices, and shortcomings of the culture are most commonly reflected in the church.

We shall cite two examples. First, scientific studies of the relationship between racial prejudice and participation in the life of the church have produced devastating results. One might expect that church members would be less prejudiced than non-members. But several studies have demonstrated that church members in general are no less and, indeed, frequently more prejudiced toward black people and Jews than non-members.[2] Two vivid quotations cry out:

> It is a well established fact that, on the average, churchgoers in our country harbor more racial, ethnic, and religious prejudice than do non-churchgoers.[3]

86

What, indeed, is the religious imperative to practice tolerance or equality, much less love, for 50 percent of the Catholics, 55 percent of the Baptists, and 62 percent of the Lutherans who think that God is more concerned with attendance at church than He is with the treatment of men? What for the Southern Baptists, almost three times as many of whom think that cursing will keep God's chillun out of heaven as those who think anti-Semitism will? [4]

Not only is this shocking from the point of view of what we as the church claim to be; it also means that the church is poorly equipped to be the instrument of change in race relations.

Second, a now classical study by Will Herberg has demonstrated that the values which are upheld by American religious institutions — Protestant, Catholic, and Jewish — are really the values of the "American Way of Life." For example, the question was asked when one ought to obey the biblical commandment to love one's neighbor. The proper response, one would think, is that one *ought* always obey it, even if we know that we don't. But the actual responses were quite different, and illuminating. Only 27 percent thought one ought to obey the law of love when the person to be loved was a member of a "dangerous political party." When the person to be loved was an "enemy of the nation," only 25 percent thought one ought to love him.[5] What this suggests is that primary loyalty is being given, *not* to the love commandment, but to the "American Way of Life." For when one thinks that a person is a threat to the "American Way of Life," one no longer, apparently, thinks that one ought to love him. Hence the church again reflects the values of the culture in which it lives, even when those values are demonstrably at variance with the Hebrew-Christian tradition.

This is not a new phenomenon, nor a strictly American one. Writing about the relationship of the church to the deplorable conditions of the working man in 19th century Europe, a distinguished Christian missionary states:

. . . when we have said the best we can, it remains true that from the point of view of the working man "the

87

*Church" in almost every country in Europe was on the
wrong side.*[6]

In that case, the church reflected the views of the dominant classes in society.

It would be bad enough if the church simply reflected
the values of society; what is even more reprehensible
is the fact that it normally *endorses* or *sanctifies* those
values as well. Historians of culture and religion have
long observed that one of the basic functions of religion
is to cement society together, to bless it, to pronounce
it "O.K.," to assure people that the society in which
they live is indeed meaningful. This can be seen in the
combination of religion with official national occasions
as, for example, in the presidential inauguration. What
ought to surprise us at least mildly is not that our presi-
dents may be religious, but that in almost every country,
the religion of that country is invoked on national occasions. Religion pronounces its blessing, sanctifying the
present order. In fairness, this charge can be made against
almost every religion; what ought to be morally shocking
to us is that Christianity is normally made to function
in the same way.

To be sure, there are enormous pressures put on the
church to conform to the biases and values of the culture
in which it lives. All of us, as mentioned earlier, breathe
deeply of our culture, and we may in all sincerity believe
that some specific cultural value is in fact a Christian
value. Not only that, but the clergy are in an unenviable
position. In most Protestant denominations, they are
subject to pressures, both psychological and financial,
from their congregations. They can be "removed" if they
take a stand that is too unpopular, and one cannot fault
them for sometimes lacking the moral courage that we
also lack. There is also the pressure from outside the
church; most of those outside certainly do not expect the
church to be an agent of change.

We need to recognize the liabilities which the church
has, and not speak too glibly about the church as the
solution, as if the church were a pure sheep in the midst
of a wolfish society. The church is part of the problem, as
well as potentially a solution. Recognizing this, what

then can we say about the way in which the church can both change itself and change society?

The church has some very real assets. To begin with the obvious, the church does have one of the most widespread local organizations in the world, perhaps even more omnipresent than Coca-Cola, which is no small feat. In the United States alone there are approximately 320,000 congregations. This means that the church can be in touch with every area in a way in which most other institutions cannot be. The potential is immense. There also are many dedicated individuals within these congregations with diverse talents that can be tapped. The church is also an international organization, transcending national and ideological barriers that no other institution does. One need only attend a Papal audience to realize this, or to reflect upon the fact that there are churches in China, North Vietnam, and Cuba, countries with which we have no official diplomatic relations. Finally, and most importantly, there is the biblical tradition upon which we are founded, a tradition that provides the most radical correction, criticism, and hope to those who affirm it. What then should the church be doing? Or, to put it more concretely, what should be happening in our local congregations?

The church exists to *celebrate* the grace of God. That is, the church is to tell the story of God's mighty acts in history, through preaching, the liturgy, and the sacraments.

But it also needs to *reflect* on and *analyze* the meaning of God's gracious acts. The local congregation should be engaged in discussion and indeed controversy within itself about what it ought to be up to in the world. If this is to succeed, it means reflection on very specific issues rather than general statements that cause offense to nobody. For example, in the local parish, questions on the relationship of Christian faithfulness to such issues as black power, interracial marriage, world hunger, war, and poverty must be faced. And they cannot be relegated to a minor position in the church's activity, where they involve only those who are already interested. What needs to be done is to confront all of us who would rather not be confronted. If the *only* place where such confrontation can occur is in the Sunday morning service, then so be it. It will at least get us talking to each other, and we need desperately to talk to each other.

That this may well involve conflict and controversy among church members is quite clear, but conflict within the church can be a source of invigoration, renewal, and reformation. If we seek to avoid conflict in order to insure some sort of artificial tranquility, then hope of renewal is surely dead. But if we wisely see in conflict the activity of God, calling us to respond, then we have come a long way.

Besides celebration and reflection, there is a third stage: action. What concrete action should be undertaken by local congregations in conflict and social change? The answer varies. In some situations, where no action group exists, the church as an institution may well decide that it needs to undertake action. In other situations, there may already be action-oriented groups which it would be redundant for the church to imitate. In such a case, Christians might well decide to affiliate with or support "secular" movements which aim at achieving similar goals, while continuing, of course, to participate in the congregational acts of celebration and reflection. There seems to be no valid reason, for example, for a "Christian" Poor People's Campaign as well as a "secular" one. Surely Christians can make common cause with "secular" movements seeking the same goals.

The thesis of this book has been that we live in a time of crisis, of conflict within the church and the world. In that crisis, the Christian has a twofold responsibility, to the church and to the world. The conflict within the church can lead to renewal or to further polarization and hardening of the moral arteries; it depends upon whether or not the conflict is dealt with wisely. For the world, the stakes are as high or higher. The result of ignoring or repressing conflict is certain and greater conflict later. If we misunderstand or mishandle the conflicts we face, the result will be greater chaos and suffering. But if conflict is faced, understood, and handled wisely, there is at least the possibility of a new order, of wholeness, of reconciliation. Such is the task of our time.

NOTES

CHAPTER 1

1. J. Brooke Mosley, *Christians in the Technical and Social Revolutions of Our Time* (Cincinnati: Forward Movement Publications, 1966), p. 119.

2. Michael Harrington, *The Accidental Century* (London: Weidenfeld and Nicholson, 1965), pp. 23-24.

3. *Wall Street Journal,* May 12, 1965.

4. No claim is being made that the framers of the Declaration of Independence meant this statement in a universal sense, or that the American experience embodies the living-out of the statement. Indeed, as many historians have noted, the statement was understood to exclude black people by many of the signers of both the Declaration and the later Constitution. Nevertheless, the statement itself was a radical one, with logical implications that reach beyond the framers' probable intent.

5. For a sobering account of the psychologically dehumanizing consequences of oppression, see especially Frantz Fanon, *The Wretched of the Earth* (New York: Grove Press,

1968), pp. 249-310; and William H. Grier and Price M. Cobbs, *Black Rage* (New York: Basic Books, Inc., 1968).

6. Carl Oglesby and Richard Shaull, *Containment and Change* (New York: Macmillan, 1967), p. 224.

CHAPTER 2

1. C. Wright Mills, quoted in Robert Lee and Martin Marty (ed.), *Religion and Social Conflict* (New York: Oxford University Press, 1964), p. 7.

2. Karl Fleming, "The Square American Speaks Out," *Newsweek,* Oct. 6, 1969, p. 33.

3. Lee and Marty, pp. 4, 55.

4. W. W. Schroeder and Victor Obenhaus, *Religion in American Culture* (London: Free Press of Glencoe, 1964), p. 160.

5. *Ibid.,* p. 174.

6. *Ibid.,* p. 182.

7. Fleming, p. 32.

8. Schroeder and Obenhaus, p. 55.

9. A. Herzog, *The Church Trap* (New York: Macmillan, 1968), pp. 45-46.

10. See, e.g., Ralf Dahrendorf, *Essays in the Theory of Society* (London: Routledge and Kegan Paul, 1968); C. Wright Mills, *Power, Politics and People* (London: Oxford University Press, 1967), pp. 525-552; Lewis Coser, *The Functions of Social Conflict* (New York: The Free Press, 1956).

11. See especially Mills.

12. *World Development: The Challenge to the Churches* (Geneva: H. Studer S.A., 1968), p. 19.

CHAPTER 3

1. For useful introductions to Amos, one might consult either J. D. Smart, "Amos," in *Interpreter's Dictionary of the Bible,* vol. 1 (New York: Abingdon Press, 1962), pp. 116-121; or A. J. Heschel, *The Prophets* (New York: Harper, 1969), pp. 27-38. Both also include extensive bibliographies for further reading.

2. Strictly speaking, it is historically incorrect to use the term "church" when referring to the eighth century before Christ. However, Amos was referring to the religious establishment of the people of God.

3. James Muilenberg, *The Way of Israel* (New York: Harper and Row, 1965), pp. 76-77. This is also an excellent introduction to the ethical implications of Old Testament thought, available in paperback.

CHAPTER 4

1. Most of this account is taken from his book *Stride Toward Freedom* (New York: Harper, 1958).

2. *Ibid.,* pp. 61-62

3. *Ibid.,* pp. 215ff. (italics not in original)

4. *Ibid.,* p. 137.

CHAPTER 5

1. Robert A. Dahl, quoted in David J. Olson, "Perspectives on Political Violence," *Dialog,* vol. 8, Winter 1969, p. 10.

2. Lewis Killian and Charles Grigg, *Racial Crisis in America* (Englewood Cliffs: Prentice Hall, Inc., 1964), p. 15.

3. Langdon Gilkey, *Shantung Compound* (New York: Harper and Row, 1966). This is an immensely readable and valuable book. Not only is it a vivid analysis of self-interest, but it also suggests the center of loyalty that makes it possible to transcend the self.

4. *Ibid.,* p. 77.

5. *Ibid.,* p. 79.

6. Reinhold Niebuhr, *The Nature and Destiny of Man,* analyzes sin as self-interest and carries his analysis into the institutionalization of self-interest. The book is now available as a two-volume paperback; volume one is most pertinent to self-interest.

7. I am indebted to Edward LeRoy Long, Jr., *A Survey of Christian Ethics* (New York: Oxford University Press, 1967), for this example.

CHAPTER 6

1. Some of this material may also be found in my article in *Discourse* magazine, Winter 1970, published by Concordia College, Moorhead, Minnesota.

2. It is proper to view the first five books of the Bible (the Pentateuch or Law) as centered on the exodus, with Genesis really being a prologue to set the stage. The next great cluster of books consists of the prophetic books, centering around the collapse of the Hebrew kingdoms and the exile. Thus we have the "Law and the Prophets." Finally, it hardly needs to be said that the whole of the New Testament draws its impetus from the career of Jesus and its consequences.

3. This is not to affirm an automatic straight-line evolutionary progress toward human perfection, as characterized the

writings of some (but not all) early twentieth century advocates of the social gospel. It is simply to affirm the virtually self-evident claim that the biblical writers view history as having a purpose and a goal.

4. In *The Book of Concord* translated and edited by Theodore G. Tappert (Philadelphia: Fortress Press, 1959), p. 365.

5. *Ibid.,* p. 366.

6. Marty and Lee, p. 173.

CHAPTER 7

1. The debate regarding a narrow versus a broad definition of conflict is summarized in Clinton Fink, "Some Conceptual Difficulties in the Theory of Social Conflict," *Journal of Conflict Resolution,* vol. 12, pp. 412-460.

2. Much of this discussion of conflict is indebted to Dahrendorf and Coser in the previously cited works.

3. Malcom Goldsmith, "Power, Authority and Conflict," in D. E. H. Whitely and R. Martin, *Sociology, Theology and Conflict* (Oxford: Basil Blackwell, 1969), p. 56.

4. King, p. 37.

5. King pp. 146, 150.

6. King, p. 187.

7. King, p. 184.

8. King, p. 86.

9. Olson, p. 17.

10. *Official Report: World Conference on Church and Society* (Geneva: World Council of Churches, 1967), p. 115.

11. *World Development: Challenge to the Churches,* p. 20.

CHAPTER 8

1. Goldsmith, p. 57

2. For a brief summary of the results of studies by Gerhard Lenski, Gordon Allport, T. W. Adorno, B'nai B'rith, and the United Church of Christ, see A. Herzog, *The Church Trap* (New York: MacMillan Co., 1968), pp. 107-111.

3. *Ibid.,* p. 107. The quotation is from Gordon Allport.

4. *Ibid.,* p. 109.

5. Will Herberg, *Protestant, Catholic and Jew* (New York: Doubleday, 1955), p. 89.

6. Stephen Neill, *The Christian Faith and Other Faiths* (New York: Oxford University Press, 1961), pp. 165.

FOR FURTHER READING

In addition to titles mentioned in the footnotes, the following are suggested to those wishing to read more. The viewpoints do not necessarily agree with each other nor with the stance developed in this book. * Denotes a book specially suited for congregational discussion.

Where to Begin (all available in paperback)

*M. Darrol Bryant. Two brief but valuable books: *To Whom It May Concern* (Philadelphia: Fortress Press, 1969); an analysis of the 1968 Poor People's Campaign, set within a theological framework. *A World Broken by Unshared Bread,* a description of the causes of, suffering due to and potential conflicts of world hunger; prepared for the 1970 Assembly of the Lutheran World Federation.

Harvey Cox. *God's Revolution and Man's Responsibility* (Valley Forge, Pa.: Judson Press). A highly readable reflection on theology and social change.

Martin Luther King. In addition to *Stride Toward Freedom* (New York: Harper & Row, 1958) his last book *Where Do*

We Go from Here: Chaos or Community? (New York: Harper & Row, 1967) is especially important.

Colin Morris. *Unyoung, Uncolored, Unpoor* (Nashville, Tenn: Abingdon Press, 1969). A highly provocative case for participation of Christians in violent revolution, in contrast to King's affirmation of nonviolence.

*Christians in the Technical and Social Revolutions of Our Time. Published by the World Council of Churches, this readable and inexpensive (25¢) book is an excellent one with which to begin

More Advanced Reading (most are available in paperback)

John Bennett, ed. *Christian Social Ethics in a Changing World* (New York: Associated Press, 1966). A collection of essays on theology and social change, including authors representing all major denominations and parts of the world.

Harvey Cox. *The Secular City* (New York: Macmillan Company, 1965). A best-selling theological analysis of the sources and implications of rapid social change.

Bruce Douglass, ed. *Reflections on Protest* (Richmond, Va: John Knox Press, 1968). Essays drawn from student involvement in social change.

Jacques Ellul. *Violence* (New York: Seabury Press, 1969). Using "violence" as a blanket term for all forms of coercion and manipulation, whether by oppressed or oppressor, he argues that violence in any form is inconsistent with the Christian faith. Includes a critique of the "theologians of revolution."

Martin Marty and Dean Peerman, ed., *New Theology No. 6* (New York: Macmillan Company). Essays on theology and revolution; sections two and three are especially germane.

Reinhold Niebuhr. Of his many books, two may be singled out: *Children of Light and Children of Darkness* (New York: Charles Scribner's Sons, 1960); *The Nature and Destiny of Man,* two volumes (New York: Charles Scribner's Sons, 1949). More technical than the other books in this list, but powerful.

Carl Oglesby and Richard Shaull. *Containment and Change* (New York: Macmillan, 1967). Oglesby's section is a penetrating analysis of the United States' relations to the Third World, especially Vietnam. Shaull's portion develops a theology of revolution.

World Council of Churches, *World Conference on Church and Society: Official Report.* The official report of the 1966 Geneva conference, which had social and technical revolutions as its theme.